WISSEN & TESTEN

Englisch

5.–7. Klasse

WISSEN & TESTEN

Englisch

5.–7. Klasse

Cornelsen
SCRIPTOR

Autoren dieses Bandes:
David Clarke und Ingrid Preedy haben langjährige Erfahrung als Englischlehrerin und -lehrer an verschiedenen Schultypen.

www.cornelsen.de

Bibliografische Information: Die Deutsche Bibliothek verzeichnet diese Publikation in der Deutschen Nationalbibliografie; detaillierte bibliografische Daten sind im Internet über http://dnb.ddb.de abrufbar.

Dieses Werk berücksichtigt die Regeln der deutschen Rechtschreibung, die seit August 2006 gelten.

1. Auflage 2010

Redaktion: Marion Clausen, Göttingen
Reihen- und Gesamtgestaltung: Dagmar & Torsten Lemme, Berlin
Druck und Bindearbeiten: CPI – Clausen & Bosse, Leck
Printed in Germany
ISBN 978-3-589-23053-2

Gedruckt auf säurefreiem Papier,
umweltschonend hergestellt aus chlorfrei gebleichten Faserstoffen.

Vorwort

Liebe Schülerin, lieber Schüler!

Die Reihe ***WISSEN & TESTEN*** informiert dich knapp und genau über das Wichtigste in einem Fach.

In übersichtlichen Lerneinheiten bekommst du auf den WISSEN-Seiten leicht verständliche Erklärungen, Regeln und Beispiele zu einem Thema. Auf den anschließenden Seiten zum TESTEN kannst du sofort überprüfen, ob du alles verstanden hast. Hier findest du Fragen und Übungen, die zu den vorigen Seiten passen. Die Antworten kannst du meist direkt auf die Seiten schreiben; wenn der Platz nicht ausreicht, verwende ein zusätzliches Blatt Papier.

Am Ende jeder Einheit stehen die Lösungen auf einem gesonderten Farbfeld, sodass du gleich kontrollieren kannst, ob du alles richtig gemacht hast. Im Inhaltsverzeichnis findest du schnell die Themen, die du gerade üben willst.
WISSEN & TESTEN Englisch erklärt den wichtigsten Stoff aus den Bereichen

- Wortarten,
- Verben und Zeitenbildung,
- Satz,

den du in den Klassen 5 bis 7 der Sekundarstufe I brauchst. Im Anhang findest du noch eine Auflistung aller grammatischen Begriffe auf Deutsch und Englisch mit Beispielen.

Mit diesem Buch kannst du dein Wissen auffrischen, dir Hilfe für Hausaufgaben oder Referate holen und testen, ob du fit für die nächste schriftliche oder mündliche Prüfung bist.

Wenn du merkst, dass dir Aufgaben noch besondere Schwierigkeiten machen, lies in deinem Schulbuch nach oder frage deine Lehrerin oder deinen Lehrer. Themen, die du noch nicht in der Schule behandelt hast (weil du zum Beispiel erst in der 5. Klasse bist), kannst du selbstverständlich überspringen und später bearbeiten.

Viel Erfolg!

INHALT

TEIL 1: WORTARTEN

TEIL 2: VERBEN

Regelmäßiger und unregelmäßiger Plural

Regelmäßiger Plural

*The **streets** of our **towns** are full of **cars.***
Die Straßen unserer Städte sind voller Autos.

*I had two **sandwiches** for lunch.*
Ich hatte zwei belegte Brote zum Mittagessen.

*A lot of **families** live in our street, but there are no **babies.***
In unserer Straße wohnen viele Familien, aber es gibt keine Babys.

*You'll find **knives** in the **boxes** at the entrance.*
Messer finden Sie in den Kästen am Eingang.

*Most cars have **radios.***
Die meisten Autos haben Radios.

*Please buy a few **potatoes.***
Kaufe bitte ein paar Kartoffeln.

Bei den weitaus meisten Nomen bilden wir den Plural mit *-s.*

Für das Anhängen von *-s* gibt es folgende Schreibregeln:
Endet der Singular auf *-ch, -s, -sh* oder *-x,* wird *-es* angehängt.

church – churches
sandwich – sandwiches
brush – brushes (Bürste)
class – classes
box – boxes

Endet der Singular auf *-y* nach einem Konsonanten, entfällt das *-y* und *-ies* wird angehängt.

baby – babies
city – cities

Endet der Singular auf *-f* bzw. *-fe*, wird *f* zu *v* und *-es* angehängt.

leaf – leaves (Blatt)
shelf – shelves (Brett)
knife – knives
life – lives

Endet der Singular auf *-o*, bilden wir den Plural mit *-s* bzw. *-es*.

photo – photos
radio – radios
potato – potatoes
tomato – tomatoes

■ Unregelmäßiger Plural

*How many **children** live here?*
Wie viele Kinder wohnen hier?

***Men** still get more money than **women**.*
Männer bekommen immer noch mehr Geld als Frauen.

*You should clean your **teeth** regularly.*
Du sollst deine Zähne regelmäßig putzen.

*Ben caught two **fish** today.*
Heute fing Ben zwei Fische.

Eine kleine Zahl von Nomen hat einen unregelmäßigen Plural.

child – children
man – men
woman – women
foot – feet
goose – geese (Gans)
tooth – teeth
mouse – mice

Beachte: Der Plural von der Maus, die du am Computer benutzt, ist:
(computer)mouse – (computer)mouses

Einige Nomen haben die gleiche Form im Singular und im Plural.
Am wichtigsten sind:

deer – deer (Hirsch)
fish – fish
fruit – fruit
sheep – sheep

Überprüfe hier, ob das Wissen sitzt

1 Bilde den Plural der unten aufgeführten Nomen.

a **At school**

chair	– ______________	desk	– ______________
girl	– ______________	pen	– ______________
shelf	– ______________	class	– ______________
felt tip	– ______________	lesson	– ______________
pencil	– ______________	table	– ______________

b **Clothes**

blouse	– ______________	dress	– ______________
pullover	– ______________	coat	– ______________
jacket	– ______________	shoe	– ______________

c **Food and drink**

apple	– ______________	cake	– ______________
drink	– ______________	potato	– ______________
sausage	– ______________	biscuit	– ______________
cheese	– ______________	orange	– ______________
sandwich	– ______________	tomato	– ______________

d **Transport**

bicycle	– ______________	car	– ______________
plane	– ______________	taxi	– ______________
van	– ______________	bus	– ______________
lorry	– ______________	ship	– ______________
train	– ______________	wheel	– ______________

2 Setze die Nomen in Klammern in der richtigen Form in den Text ein. Pass dabei gut auf, weil einige in der Einzahl bleiben müssen.

The _______________ (child) in Miss Jones' _______________ (class) are very excited *(aufgeregt)*. They are planning a class _____________ (party), and they think that _______________ (party) are great. Miss Jones is talking to the _____________ (boy) and _____________ (girl) about everything they must do. "What about _____________ (knife) and ___________ (fork)?" she says. "And who can bring some __________ (cup) and ________________ (glass)?" "I can," says Amy. Miss Jones writes down Amy's ___________ (name) on one of her __________ (list). "Now," she says, " let's talk about the ___________ (food). What would you like to have?" "Oh", says Adam, "lots of lovely ________________ (biscuit), chocolate __________ (cake) and ______________ (sweet), of course, Miss." "Don't be a silly __________ (boy), Adam," says Miss Jones. "Sweet _______________ (thing) are very bad for your _____________ (tooth)."

1 a (At school) chairs – desks – girls – pens – shelves – classes – felt tips – lessons – pencils – tables
b (Clothes) blouses – dresses – pullovers – coats – jackets – shoes
c (Food and drink) apples – cakes – drinks – potatoes – sausages – biscuits – cheeses – oranges – sandwiches – tomatoes
d (Transport) bicycles – cars – planes – taxis – vans – buses – lorries – ships – trains – wheels

2 The children in Miss Jones' class are very excited. They are planning a class party, and they think that parties are great. Miss Jones is talking to the boys and girls about everything they must do. "What about knives and forks?" she says. "And who can bring some cups and glasses?" "I can," says Amy. Miss Jones writes down Amy's name on one of her lists. "Now," she says, " let's talk about the food. What would you like to have?" "Oh", says Adam, "lots of lovely biscuits, chocolate cakes and sweets, of course, Miss." "Don't be a silly boy, Adam," says Miss Jones. "Sweet things are very bad for your teeth."

Zählbare und nichtzählbare Nomen

Zählbare Nomen

Nomen wie *rolls, apples* und *bananas* sind zählbar. Sie haben eine Pluralform und können daher mit *a/an* und Zahlwörtern benutzt werden.

Kate always has ***a roll*** *for breakfast.*
Kate isst immer ein Brötchen zum Frühstück.

I'd like ***four apples*** *and* ***six bananas,*** *please.*
Ich hätte gern vier Äpfel und sechs Bananen.

Nichtzählbare Nomen

Nomen wie *butter* und *cheese* sind dagegen nichtzählbar. Sie haben keine Pluralform und können deswegen nicht ohne Weiteres mit *a/an* oder Zahlwörtern gebraucht werden.

We need ***some butter*** *and* ***some cheese.***
Wir brauchen etwas Butter und Käse.

Wollen wir nichtzählbare Nomen im Plural dennoch benutzen, dann müssen wir ein geeignetes zählbares Nomen – z. B. *packets of* oder *slices of* – hinzufügen.
Die folgenden zählbaren Begriffe kannst du benutzen, um nichtzählbare Nomen zählbar zu machen:

a ***bar*** *of*	*chocolate*	ein Riegel/eine Tafel Schokolade
a ***bottle*** *of*	*mineral water*	eine Flasche Mineralwasser
a ***can*** *of*	*coke*	eine Dose Cola
a ***cup*** *of*	*coffee*	eine Tasse Kaffee
a ***glass*** *of*	*milk*	ein Glas Milch
a ***kilo*** *of*	*ham*	ein Kilo Schinken
a ***litre*** *of*	*apple juice*	ein Liter Apfelsaft
a ***packet*** *of*	*tea*	ein Päckchen Tee

a ***pound*** *of*	*meat*	ein Pfund Fleisch
a ***slice*** *of*	*bread*	eine Scheibe Brot
a ***tin*** *of*	*paint*	eine Dose Farbe
a ***tube*** *of*	*toothpaste*	eine Tube Zahnpasta

Please buy ***two packets of butter*** *and* ***eight slices of cheese.***
Kaufe bitte zwei Packete Butter und acht Scheiben Käse.

Die folgenden Nomen sind im Englischen – anders als im Deutschen – nichtzählbar. Daher stehen die dazugehörigen Verben und Pronomen immer im Singular:

advice	Rat, Ratschläge	*damage*	Schaden, Schäden
furniture	Möbel	*hair*	Haar(e)
homework	Hausaufgabe(n)	*housework*	Hausarbeit(en)
information	Information(en)	*news*	Nachrichten

Have you washed your ***hair*** *this week?* ***It's*** *dirty.*
Hast du deine Haare diese Woche gewaschen? Sie sind dreckig.

Überprüfe hier, ob das Wissen sitzt

1 Setze die richtige Gegenwartsform des Verbs in Klammern in die Sätze ein.

a There ________________ (be) two loaves of bread on the table.

b This bread ________________ (be) from the baker's.

c These two pieces of land ________________ (belong to) farmer Brown.

d This piece of furniture ________________ (belong to) Mr and Mrs Cobb.

e These pieces of music ________________ (be) by Händel.

f This music ________________ (sound) nice.

2 Übersetze ins Englische.

a eine Dose Cola ________________

b ein Pfund Fleisch ________________

c ein Päckchen Tee ________________

d ein Liter Apfelsaft ________________

e drei Scheiben Käse ________________

3 Kreuze die zehn nichtzählbaren Nomen an.

bike	☐	computer	☐	information	☐
boy	☐	cow	☐	mouse	☐
bread	☐	furniture	☐	news	☐
butter	☐	glass	☐	pet	☐
cat	☐	goldfish	☐	tooth	☐
chocolate	☐	hair	☐	water	☐
money	☐	homework	☐		

4 Übersetze die unterstrichenen Satzteile ins Englische.

a Die Hausaufgaben sind zu viel. ______________________

b Viele Ratschläge werden gegeben. ______________________

c Diese Schäden sind neu. ______________________

d Die Neuigkeiten waren gut. ______________________

e Es gibt keine Beweise.

____

5 Nenne vier Nomen, die im Englischen nur im Singular stehen.

______________________ ______________________

______________________ ______________________

1 a are
b is
c belong to
d belongs to
e are
f sounds

2 a a can of coke
b a pound of meat
c a packet of tea
d a litre of apple juice
e three slices of cheese

3 Nichtzählbar sind:
bread
butter
chocolate
money
furniture
hair
homework
information
news
water

4 a The homework is
b A lot of advice is
c This damage is
d The news was
e There is no evidence.

5 Beispiele:
advice
damage
hair
housework

Nomen, die nur im Plural stehen

Dinge, die aus zwei Teilen bestehen, wie *glasses,* können wir im Englischen nur im Plural benutzen.
Wollen wir solche „Paarwörter" im Singular mit *a/an* oder mit einem Zahlwort im Plural benutzen, müssen wir *a pair of* ... bzw. *two/three/* ... *pairs of* hinzufügen.

glasses	Brille
headphones	Kopfhörer
jeans	Jeans
leggings	Leggings
pants	BE: Unterhose; AE: Hose
scissors	Schere
shorts	kurze Hose, Shorts
tights	Strumpfhose
trousers	Hose

Where ***are*** *my* ***glasses****?*
Wo ist meine Brille?

He only has ***two pairs of trousers****.*
Er hat nur zwei Hosen.

Beachte, dass wir *people* (Menschen) und *police* nur im Plural benutzen.
People are *sometimes hard to understand.*
Menschen sind manchmal schwer zu verstehen.

The police are *here. They want to speak to the boss.*
Die Polizei ist hier. Sie will mit dem Chef sprechen.

Überprüfe hier, ob das Wissen sitzt

Übersetze die unterstrichenen Satzteile ins Englische.

a Bob hat eine Schere.

____

b Tom hat drei Shorts.

____

c Ich habe einen blauen Schlafanzug.

____

d Kirstys Strumpfhose ist kaputt.

____

e Das ist mein Kopfhörer.

____

f Mr Carters Brille ist schmutzig.

____

g Mr Parker besitzt drei Jeans.

____

a a pair of scissors
b three pairs of shorts
c a pair of blue pyjamas
d Kirsty's tights are
e are my headphones
f Mr Carter's glasses are
g three pairs of jeans

Die Stützwörter *one/ones*

One (Singular) und *ones* (Plural) werden verwendet, wenn man ein schon genanntes (zählbares) Nomen nicht noch einmal wiederholen will. Im Deutschen gibt es dafür keine Entsprechung.
One wird auch nach *this* und *that* gebraucht.
Nach *these* und *those* steht meistens kein Stützwort.

Beachte: Anders als im Deutschen kann ein Adjektiv nicht allein stehen.
Do you want ***the blue shirt*** *or* ***the yellow one****?*
Willst du das blaue Hemd oder das gelbe?

I'd like three ***white candles*** *and two* ***red ones,*** *please.*
Ich möchte drei weiße Kerzen und zwei rote, bitte.

Überprüfe hier, ob das Wissen sitzt

Ersetze die unterstrichenen Nomen durch das Stützwort *one* oder *ones*.

a I don't like all of these baseball caps. I like the blue cap and the red caps.

____

____

b Tom has a brown football and a white football.

____

c These books are not as good as the books I borrowed last week.

____

____

d I think this CD is better than that CD.

____

e Amy has got a pair of blue jeans and a pair of black jeans.

____

____

f These apples are good, but the apples we bought yesterday were better.

____

____

a I like the blue one and the red ones.
b Tom has a brown football and a white one.
c These books are not as good as the ones I borrowed last week.
d I think this CD is better than that one.
e Amy has got a pair of blue jeans and a pair of black ones.
f These apples are good, but the ones we bought yesterday were better.

5

Der Genitiv

■ 's-Genitiv

Bei Personen und Tieren mit Namen benutzen wir den *'s*-Genitiv.
Ist das Nomen im Singular oder endet der Plural nicht auf *-s*, dann hängen wir einfach *-'s* an.
Endet der Plural auf *-s*, dann hängen wir einfach ein Apostroph (') an.

***Cathy's room** is too small.*
Cathys Zimmer ist zu klein.

*Do you sell **children's clothes**?*
Verkaufen Sie Kinderbekleidung?

*This is **Tiger's** cushion.*
Dies ist Tigers Kissen.

*The **girls'** and the **boys'** team both won.*
Die Mädchen- und die Jungenmannschaft haben beide gewonnen.

Beachte diese Besonderheiten:

- Haben wir das dazugehörige Nomen schon genannt, steht der *'s*-Genitiv meist allein:
  Who does this book belong to? *It is **Cathy's**.*
  Wem gehört dieses Buch? Es ist Cathys.
- Bei Geschäften lassen wir das Nomen grundsätzlich weg:
  *I saw Tim **at the baker's.*** Nicht: *baker's shop*
  Ich habe Tim beim Bäcker gesehen.

  *We always buy our meat **at the butcher's.*** Nicht: *butcher's shop*
  Wir kaufen unser Fleisch immer beim Metzger.
- Bei diesen Zeitangaben benutzen wir auch den *'s*-Genitiv:

***an hour's** wait*	*eine Wartezeit von einer Stunde*
***last year's** calendar*	*der Kalender vom letzten Jahr*
***tonight's** TV programme*	*das Fernsehprogramm für heute Abend*
***today's** newspaper*	*die heutige Zeitung*
***this week's** weather*	*das Wetter von dieser Woche*

■ *of*-Genitiv

Bei Sachen benutzen wir den *of*-Genitiv.

The price of the flat *was too high.*
Der Preis der Wohnung war zu hoch.

The children were playing in ***the middle of the road.***
Die Kinder spielten mitten auf der Straße.

The man opened ***the door of the car*** *without looking.*
Der Mann öffnete die Autotür ohne zu schauen.

Überprüfe hier, ob das Wissen sitzt

1 Verbinde Wörter aus der rechten Liste mit einem Begriff aus der linken Liste wie im Beispiel.

dog	*Amy's dog*	Amy
sweets		Adam
bus		Miss Jones
football		Mr Clarke
cage		Mrs Nunn
bicycle		Bob and Tom
car		Tweets *(Vogel)*
bag		the wheel

2 Übersetze die unterstrichenen Teile der Sätze ins Englische.

a Wir spielen oft im <u>Garten meiner Eltern</u>.

b <u>Amys Hund</u>, Spooky, und <u>Mrs Cobbs Vogel</u>, Tweets, mögen gern Schokolade.

c Mr Parker streicht <u>das Fenster von Bobs Zimmer</u>.

d <u>Adams Haus</u> ist am <u>Ende der Straße</u>.

e Toms Mathebuch ist dreckig und sechs Seiten des Buches fehlen.

f Die Farbe seiner Augen ist grün.

g Der Name von Kirstys Hund ist Archie.

1 Beispiele (die Begriffe können auch anders zusammengeführt werden):
Adam's sweets
Miss Jones' bag
Mr Clarke's car
the wheel of the bike (bicycle)
Bob and Tom's football
Mrs Nunn's bus
Tweets' cage

2 a my parents' garden
b Amy's dog – Mrs Cobb's bird
c the window of Bob's room
d Adam's house – end of the street
e Tom's maths book – six pages of the book
f The colour of his eyes
g The name of Kirsty's dog is Archie.

6

Der bestimmte Artikel

***The boys** in our road are nice.*
Die Jungen in unserer Straße sind nett.

***The apples** and **the oranges** are bad.*
Die Äpfel und die Orangen sind faul.

■ Form

Die Form des bestimmten Artikels *the* bleibt immer dieselbe.
Die Aussprache ändert sich wie folgt:
Beginnt das Wort unmittelbar nach dem Artikel mit einem ausgesprochenen Konsonanten (*b, c, d, f* usw.), dann wird das *e* in *the* wie das *e* in „Schule" ausgesprochen.
Beginnt das Wort direkt nach dem Artikel mit einem ausgesprochenen Vokal (*a, e, i* usw.), dann wird das *e* in *the* wie das *ie* in „Biene" ausgesprochen.

■ Gebrauch

Reden wir nur über bestimmte Personen oder Sachen, benutzen wir den bestimmten Artikel. Reden wir über alle Personen oder Sachen ohne Ausnahme, dann lassen wir den bestimmten Artikel weg.

***Cats** are nice animals.* Katzen sind nette Tiere.	Alle Katzen ohne Ausnahme sind nett, also kein *the*.
***The cats** I know are nice.* Die Katzen, die ich kenne, sind nett.	Nur diese Katzen sind nett, also benutzen wir *the*.

■ Abweichungen zwischen Englisch und Deutsch

Ohne *the:*

- Straßennamen
  *The nearest supermarket is in **Park Street.***
  Der nächste Supermarkt ist in der Parkstraße.
- Verkehrsmittel
  *Frank often goes **by train.***
  Frank fährt oft mit dem Zug.

It's quicker ***by bus.***
Es ist schneller mit dem Bus.

- die meisten öffentlichen Gebäude
  My mother is ***in hospital.***
  Meine Mutter liegt im Krankenhaus.

  His father ist ***in prison.***
  Sein Vater ist im Gefängnis.

  Tim and Frank are ***at school.***
  Tim und Frank sind in der Schule.

- kein *the* mit *town* als Ortsangabe
  I saw Cathy ***in town*** *today.*
  Ich sah Cathy heute in der Stadt.

- Mahlzeiten
  What do you have ***for breakfast****?*
  Was isst du zum Frühstück?

  I must go shopping ***after lunch****.*
  Nach dem Mittagessen muss ich einkaufen gehen.

- *most* im Sinne von „die meisten"
  Most people *are friendly.*
  Die meisten Menschen sind freundlich.

- kein *the* mit TV
  I often ***watch TV.***
  Ich sehe oft fern.

Mit *the:*

- Radio
  I often listen ***to the radio.***
  Ich höre oft Radio.

- Musikinstrumente
  Chiara can play ***the violin.***
  Chiara kann Geige spielen.

■ Überprüfe hier, ob das Wissen sitzt

1 Unterstreiche den bestimmten Artikel, bei dem du das *e* wie das *ie* in „Liebe" aussprechen musst.

the airport; the aunt; the bottle; the cat; the CD; the egg; the English book; the exercise; the flower; the garden; the hospital; the house; the ice cream; the invitation; the jeans; the new school; the old town; the CD player; the taxi driver; the uncle.

2 Setze den bestimmten Artikel nur dann ein, wenn es nötig ist.

a Kirsty doesn't live in __________ Oak Lane. She lives in *the* white house at __________ end of __________ Cherry Tree Road.

b __________ most/Most of __________ boys at __________ Green Park School like __________ football, but a lot of __________ girls think that basketball or volleyball is more fun.

c – Do you go to __________ school by bus or by train?
– Well, I go by __________ taxi. __________ taxi/Taxi belongs to my dad.

d – Should we go to __________ town today? __________ film/ Film about the Eskimos is on at _____ cinema in _____ Station Road.
– Yes, OK. We can go by __________ bike.

3 Übersetze ins Englische.

a Die Vereinigten Staaten ______________________

b Der Südwesten ______________________

c Vor dem Sturm ______________________

d Am Abend ______________________

e Mit dem Fahrrad ______________________

f Nach dem Frühstück ______________________

g Ich mag Blumen. ______________________

h Er studiert Geschichte. ______________________

i Meine Mutter mag Milch. ______________________

j Ich besuche oft Onkel John. ______________________

k Tim geht sonntags in die Kirche. ______________________

1 (the airport) – the aunt – the egg – the English book – the exercise – the ice cream – the invitation – the old town – the uncle

2 a Kirsty doesn't live in Oak Lane. She lives in (the) white house at the end of Cherry Tree Road.
b Most of the boys at Green Park School like football, but a lot of the girls think that basketball oder volleyball ist more fun.
c – Do you go to school by bus or by train?
– Well, I go by taxi. The taxi belongs to my dad, you see.
d – Should we go to town today? The film about the Eskimos is on at the cinema in Station Road.
– Yes, OK. We can go by bike.

3 a The United States
b The South-West
c Before the storm
d In the evening
e By bicycle
f After breakfast
g I like flowers.
h He studies history.
i My mother likes milk.
j I often visit uncle John.
k Tim goes to church on Sundays.

7

Der unbestimmte Artikel

Form

Die Form des unbestimmten Artikels ist immer entweder *a* oder *an.*
Die Schreibweise ändert sich wie folgt:
Beginnt das Wort unmittelbar nach dem unbestimmten Artikel mit einem Konsonanten, dann benutzen wir *a.* Beginnt aber das Wort mit einem ausgesprochenen Vokal, benutzen wir *an.*

Entscheidend ist, wie wir den Anfangslaut des Wortes aussprechen, also nicht, wie wir ihn schreiben. Das Wort *hour* z.B. wird ohne *h* gesprochen, also gilt der Wortanfang als Vokal.

*Cathy has **a cat.***
Cathy hat eine Katze.

*Tim wants **an apple.***
Tim will einen Apfel.

*I waited for **an hour.***
Ich wartete eine Stunde.

*German schools don't have **a uniform.***
An deutschen Schulen gibt es keine Uniform.

Gebrauch

Der unbestimmte Artikel *a/an* bedeutet so viel wie „eins". Daher können wir ihn nur mit zählbaren Nomen im Singular benutzen.

Abweichungen zwischen Englisch und Deutsch

Anders als im Deutschen verwenden wir im Englischen den unbestimmten Artikel *(a/an)* in folgenden Fällen:

- bei Berufsangaben
  *She's **an engineer** and he's **a nurse.***
  Sie ist Ingenieurin und er ist Krankenpfleger.

- bei leichteren Krankheiten
  *Cathy has **a cold.***
  Cathy ist erkältet.

I have ***a stomach ache.***
Ich habe Bauchweh.

Tim has ***a sore throat*** *today.*
Tim hat heute Halsschmerzen.

Beachte die Ausnahmen:

- kein *a* mit Ohren-/Zahnschmerzen
  He has ***earache/toothache.***
  Er hat Ohrschmerzen/Zahnschmerzen.

- bei Nationalitäten und Religionen
  Is Anna ***an Austrian*** *oder* ***a German****?*
  Ist Anna Österreicherin oder Deutsche?

  Ali is ***a Muslim.***
  Ali ist Muslim.

- bei Mengen- und Zeitangaben
  These apples cost ***$ 2 a bag.***
  Diese Äpfel kosten $ 2 pro Tüte.

  We have English ***three times a week.***
  Wir haben dreimal die Woche Englisch.

Beachte die folgenden Wendungen:

I am in a hurry.	Ich bin in Eile.
Cathy is having a shower/wash.	Cathy duscht/wäscht sich gerade.
Can she ride a bike?	Kann sie Fahrrad fahren?
They often go for a walk.	Sie gehen oft spazieren.
What a pity!	Wie schade!
I had to wait for a long time.	Ich musste lange warten.
The bus left at a quarter to one.	Der Bus fuhr um Viertel vor eins.

Überprüfe hier, ob das Wissen sitzt

1 Setze *a* oder *an* vor den Wörtern ein.

__a__ man; __an__ old book; _____ accident; _____ address; _____ bag;

_____ cake; _____ DVD player; _____ dirty shoe; _____ egg;

_____ English book; _____ expensive T-shirt; _____ family; _____ flat;

_____ guitar; _____ hand; _____ hotel; _____ hour; _____ idea;

_____ CD; _____ magazine; _____ mistake; _____ noise; _____ old car;

_____ orange; _____ pen; _____ pet; _____ question; _____ uncle;

_____ underground train; _____ uniform; _____ untidy room;

_____ village; _____ wall; _____ year; _____ yellow apple; _____ zoo

2 Übersetze die unterstrichenen Teile der Sätze ins Englische.

a Mrs Nunn ist Busfahrerin.

____

b Bob hat Kopfschmerzen und Adam ist erkältet.

____

c Tom ist so langsam. Wir sind in Eile.

____

d Kann Mr Parker Fahrrad fahren?

____

e Wir warten immer lange Zeit auf den Bus.

____

f Kirsty hat eine Uniform, aber sie zieht sie nie an.

____

g Es ist jetzt Viertel vor acht.

____

h Wie schade! Der Fernseher ist kaputt.

____

i Tom duscht gerade.

____

j Amy will Lehrerin werden, wenn sie groß ist.

____

1 (a) man – (an) old book – an accident – an address – a bag – a cake – a DVD player – a dirty shoe – an egg – an English book – an expensive T-shirt – a family – a flat – a guitar – a hand – a hotel – an hour – an idea – a CD – a magazine – a mistake – a noise – an old car – an orange – a pen – pet – question – an uncle – an underground train – a uniform – an untidy room – a village – a wall – a year – a yellow apple – a zoo

2
a is a bus driver
b has (got) a headache – has (got) a cold
c in a hurry/in a rush
d ride a bike
e a long time
f has (got) a uniform
g (a) quarter to eight
h What a pity!
i is showering/is having a shower
j wants to be a teacher/wants to become a teacher

8

Der bestimmte Artikel bei abstrakten Nomen

Wenn wir sie im allgemeinen Sinn benutzen, stehen abstrakte Nomen, die Ideen bzw. geistige Konzepte benennen, ohne bestimmten Artikel.
Life *is hard without money.*
Das Leben ist hart ohne Geld.

Wenn sie näher bestimmt sind, stehen abstrakte Nomen mit bestimmtem Artikel.
The life *of the poor is hard.*
Das Leben der Armen ist hart.

Das gilt auch, wenn die abstrakten Nomen Stoffe und Materialien bezeichnen.
We can't live without ***water.***
Ohne Wasser können wir nicht leben.

The water *in the North Sea is dirty.*
Das Wasser in der Nordsee ist dreckig.

Überprüfe hier, ob das Wissen sitzt

Setze den bestimmten Artikel *the* nur dann ein, wenn er unbedingt notwendig ist.

a We don't pay enough for ________ food we get from ________ poor farmers in Africa.

b One of ________ biggest problems in our cities is ________ crime.

c Do ________ football players really earn ________ money they get from ________ TV?

d Is it true that ________ bears can live ________ weeks without ________ food?

e As ________ skiing is so important in ________ Alps, they need ________ snow in ________ winter.

f Some say that ________ girls are better at ________ languages than ________ boys, but ________ girls in my class are no better than ________ boys.

a We don't pay enough for the food we get from poor farmers in Africa.
b One of the biggest problems in our cities is crime.
c Do football players really earn the money they get from TV?
d Is it true that bears can live weeks without food?
e As skiing is so important in the Alps, they need snow in winter.
f Some say that girls are better at languages than boys, but the girls in my class are no better than the boys.

9

Die Personalpronomen

Personalpronomen können Nomen ersetzen. Wir benutzen sie unter anderem, um eine eintönige Wiederholung von Namen und Nomen zu vermeiden.
Im Englischen – ganz anders als im Deutschen – benutzen wir immer *it* für Sachen und Tiere.
Die geschlechtsanzeigenden Pronomen *he* und *she* werden nur für Menschen und Haustiere verwendet.
Personalpronomen können sowohl Subjekt als auch Objekt eines Satzes sein.

■ **Subjektform *(Subject form)***

Tim *likes sport.* ***He*** *is a good basketball player.*
Tim mag Sport. Er ist ein guter Basketballspieler.

Cathy *likes sport, too.* ***She*** *is a good swimmer.*
Auch Cathy mag Sport. Sie ist eine gute Schwimmerin.

Look at that ***cow. It*** *can hardly walk.*
Schau dir die Kuh an. Sie kann kaum laufen.

Tim and Frank *aren't here.* ***They*** *are ill.*
Tim und Frank sind nicht hier. Sie sind krank.

■ **Objektform *(Object form)***

This car nearly hit ***me****.*
Dieses Auto hat mich fast angefahren.

Cathy: Where's ***Mary?*** *Tim: No idea. I haven't seen* ***her*** *today.*
Cathy: Wo ist Mary? Tim: Keine Ahnung. Ich habe sie heute nicht gesehen.

Can you lend ***me*** *your* ***English book?*** *I'll bring* ***it*** *back tomorrow.*
Kannst du mir dein Englischbuch ausleihen? Ich bringe es morgen zurück.

Hier sind zwei Listen der englischen Personalpronomen mit ihren deutschen Bedeutungen. Wie du siehst, gibt es im Englischen keine höfliche Sie-Form.

Subjektform	
I	ich
you	du/Sie
he	er
she	sie
it	es
we	wir
you	ihr/Sie
they	sie

Objektform (wem?, wen? oder was?)	
me	mich/mir
you	dich/dir, Sie/Ihnen
him	ihn/ihm
her	sie/ihr
it	ihn/ihm, sie/ihr, es/ihm
us	uns/uns
you	euch/Sie, euch/Ihnen
them	sie/ihnen

■ Überprüfe hier, ob das Wissen sitzt

1 Ersetze alle Subjekte mit Pronomen in der Subjektform. Trage die Pronomen rechts ein.

a Tom goes to school by bike. *he*

b Amy has cornflakes for breakfast. ______

c Kirsty has got some new shoes. ______

d The Rolls-Royce is standing in front of the house. ______

e Bob, Tom and Adam all live in Oak Lane. ______

f Miss Jones teaches in Kingston. ______

g Fiats and Ferraries are cars from Italy. ______

2 Ersetze alle unterstrichenen Objekte mit Pronomen in der Objektform. Trage die Pronomen rechts ein.

a We all like <u>Miss Jones</u>. *her*

b The dog is running after <u>Adam</u>. ______

c My mother is visiting <u>Mr and Mrs Parker</u>. ______

d The boys are meeting <u>Kirsty and Amy</u>. ______

e The policeman is stopping <u>the BMW</u> in King Street. ______

f Bob is giving Amy <u>a box of chocolates</u>. ______

g Mr Carter teaches <u>the boys and girls</u> maths. ______

3 Trage die fehlenden Pronomen sowohl in der Subjektform als auch in der Objektform ein.

My mother is meeting the girls. ________ are in the shop.

My mother is talking to ________ . ________ are telling ________ that

________ are looking for a present for Adam.

But ________ don't know what to buy ________ . My mother says to

________ that she thinks it's a good idea to get ________ a CD, but the

girls say ________ don't want to buy a CD. ________ think ________ is

too expensive. Amy says ________ thinks that a cap is a good idea, but

Kirsty thinks ________ is a silly idea. ________ says Adam already has a

cap, and ________ doesn't like ________ .

Suddenly Adam comes into the shop. " ________ know that ________

are talking about ________ ", ________ says.

"________ don't know what to buy ________ for my birthday.

Well, ________ want lots of sweets for my birthday. ________ know

how much ________ love ________ ."

1 a he b she c she d it e they f she g they

2 a her b him c them d them e it f her g them

3 My mother is meeting the girls. They are in the shop. My mother is talking to them. They are telling her that they are looking for a present for Adam. But they don't know what to buy him. My mother says to them that she thinks it's a good idea to get him a CD, but the girls say they don't want to buy a CD. They think it is too expensive. Amy says she thinks that a cap is a good idea, but Kirsty thinks it is a silly idea. She says Adam already has a cap, and he doesn't like it. Suddenly Adam comes into the shop. „I know that you are talking about me", he says. „You don't know what to buy me for my birthday. Well, I want lots of sweets for my birthday. You know how much I love them."

10

Die Possessivbegleiter und Possessivpronomen

Die Possessivbegleiter

Die Possessivbegleiter sagen uns, wem irgendetwas gehört.
Im Englischen wie im Deutschen stehen Possessivbegleiter unmittelbar vor dem dazugehörigen Nomen.

*Have you seen **my** new bike?*
Hast du mein neues Fahrrad gesehen?

*Where is **your** Englisch book, Tim?*
Wo ist dein Englischbuch, Tim?

*Cathy lost **her** mobile yesterday.*
Cathy hat gestern ihr Handy verloren.

*The horse loves **its** owner.*
Das Pferd liebt seinen Besitzer.

*Tiger is **our** cat.*
Tiger ist unsere Katze.

*The Greens often work in **their** garden.*
Die Greens arbeiten oft in ihrem Garten.

Hier ist eine Liste der Possessivbegleiter:

Personalpronomen	Possessivbegleiter
I	*my*
you	*your*
he	*his*
she	*her*
it	*its*
we	*our*
you	*your*
they	*their*

Beachte die Schreibweise von *its* und *their*. *Its* wird manchmal mit *it's* – also der Kurzform von *it is* – verwechselt und *their* mit *there* (da/dort).

Die Possessivpronomen

*This coat is **mine**, not yours.*
Dieser Mantel ist meiner, nicht deiner.

*Is this **your** book, Tim? – No, it's **his**.*
Ist dies dein Buch, Tim? – Nein, es ist seins.

*The Greens' garden is much bigger than **ours**.*
Der Garten der Greens ist viel größer als unserer.

*Tiger is nicer than **their** cat. **Theirs** is nasty.*
Tiger ist netter als ihre Katze. Ihre ist böse.

Possessivpronomen wie *mine, hers* usw. stehen allein, also ohne Nomen.

Wir benutzen Possessivpronomen statt eines schon erwähnten Possessivbegleiters + Nomen, um eintönige Wiederholungen zu vermeiden.
Hier ist eine Liste der Possessivpronomen:

Personalpronomen	Possessivpronomen
I	*mine*
you	*yours*
he	*his*
she	*hers*
it	–
we	*ours*
you	*yours*
they	*theirs*

10

Überprüfe hier, ob das Wissen sitzt

1 Trage die fehlenden Possessivbegleiter ein.

Amy is going to a disco with ________ friend Kirsty. ________ boyfriend Bob is there, too. " ________ dress is lovely," he says to Amy. The song playing is by "The Chinks". Tom loves ________ music. He always plays ________ songs at home and annoys ________ parents. Amy listens to ________ CDs sometimes. But ________ favourite singer is Robbie Williams. They are dancing but the music is too loud. "________ ears hurt," says Kirsty, "and ________ feet are sore."

2 Übersetze die unterstrichenen Teile der Sätze ins Englische.

a Tom bekommt einen Fußball zu *(for)* seinem Geburtstag. Seine Schwester gibt ihm ein Buch.

____

b Mrs Nunn räumt ihren Bus jeden Abend auf.

____

c Adam versteckt seine Bonbons unter seinem Schreibtisch. Sie liegen auf seinem Englischbuch.

____

d Der arme Vogel hat sich den Flügel *(wing)* gebrochen.

____

e Kleine Kinder tragen ihre Schultaschen *(school bag)* auf dem Rücken *(back)*, weil sie sehr schwer sind.

____

f Kirsty packt ihre Tasche.

____

3 Trage die fehlenden Possessivbegleiter und -pronomen ein.

a Cathy is going dancing with __________ friend Frank tonight.

b Tim likes Crazy Wizards. He's listening to __________ new CD.

c Frank wants __________ sister to help him.

d That poor cow has hurt __________ leg.

e I hurt __________ arm in the volleyball game.

f "Hey, boy, what is __________ name?" shouts the teacher.

g Is this your shoe? Yes, it's __________ .

h Is this __________ coat, Helen? No, its not __________ .

Ask Sally. It must be __________ .

1 Amy is going to a disco with her friend Kirsty. Her boyfriend Bob is there, too. „Your dress is lovely," he says to Amy. The song playing is by „The Chinks". Tom loves their music. He always plays their songs at home and annoys his parents. Amy listens to their CDs sometimes. But her favourite singer is Robbie Williams. They are dancing but the music is too loud. „My ears hurt," says Kirsty, „and my feet are sore."

2 a for his birthday – His sister
b her bus
c his sweets – his desk – his English book
d its wing
e their school bags – their backs
f her bag

3 a her
b their
c his
d its
e my
f your
g mine
h your – mine – hers

Die Demonstrativpronomen

This (Singular) und *these* (Plural) benutzen wir bei Personen und Dingen, die in unserer Nähe sind.
This bike *(here) belongs to Cathy.*
Dieses Rad (hier) gehört Cathy.

These CDs *(here) are cheaper.*
Diese CDs (hier) sind billiger.

That (Singular) und *those* (Plural) dagegen benutzen wir bei weiter entfernten Personen und Dingen.
That woman *(over there) is a teacher.*
Diese Frau (dort drüben) ist Lehrerin.

Those girls *(over there) are in my class.*
Diese Mädchen (dort drüben) sind in meiner Klasse.

Überprüfe hier, ob das Wissen sitzt

1 Trage die fehlenden Demonstrativpronomen ein.

a ___________ books (here) all belong to me.

b ___________ plant (here) needs some water.

c ___________ black dog (over there) is Luna.

d ___________ jeans (over there) are quite cheap.

e We must wait at ___________ bus-stop (over there) for the 371.

2 Setze jeweils ein Demonstrativpronomen ein.

a Is _this_ your dog here?

b No, _that_ is my dog over there.

c Who is ___________ man over there?

d Which man? Oh, ________ man. ________ is Mr Carter.

e Which shoes do you think I should buy, ________ blue ones here or ________ red ones over there?

f ________ sweets I'm eating are great!

g Look here, boys and girls. I've got ________ test. Whose is it?

h ________ is my test, Miss Jones.

i No, Tom. ________ isn't your test. ________ is your test over there.

j But isn't ________ your writing, Amy? I think ________ is your test.

k No, Miss Jones. ________ is not my test. ________ is my test. I have it in my hand.

1 a	These	2 a	(this)	g	this
b	This	b	(that)	h	That
c	That	c	that	i	this – That
d	Those	d	that – that	j	this – this
e	that	e	these – those	k	That – This
		f	These		

TESTEN • TESTEN • TESTEN • TESTEN • TESTEN • TESTEN • TESTEN • TESTEN • TESTEN

12

Die *self*-Pronomen

Self-Pronomen beziehen sich auf das Subjekt des Satzes. Wir verwenden sie also, wenn Subjekt und Objekt identisch sind.
*Mum **cut herself** when she was opening a can.*
Mama hat sich geschnitten, als sie eine Dose öffnete.

*Babies **can't look after themselves.***
Babys können nicht für sich selbst sorgen.

Im Englischen verwenden wir *self*-Pronomen auch, wenn wir verdeutlichen wollen, dass das Subjekt des Satzes irgendetwas selbst tut oder getan hat. Bei diesem Gebrauch verwenden wir im Deutschen „selbst" bzw. „selber".
*Jack Hooper **made** this table **himself.***
Jack Hooper machte diesen Tisch selbst.

*We **can't repair** the computer **ourselves.***
Wir können den Computer nicht selbst reparieren.

■ Übersicht der *self*-Pronomen

I	*myself*
you	*yourself*
he	*himself*
she	*herself*
it	*itself*
we	*ourselves*
you	*yourselves*
they	*themselves*

Die folgenden geläufigen deutschen Verben werden im Englischen ohne *self*-Pronomen verwendet:

sich ändern	*change*
sich beeilen	*hurry*
sich beklagen	*complain*
sich bewegen	*move*
sich duschen	*shower*
sich erinnern	*remember*
sich entschuldigen	*apologise*
sich entspannen	*relax*
sich fragen	*wonder*
sich freuen auf	*look forward to*
sich fühlen	*feel*
sich fürchten	*be afraid*
sich hinlegen	*lie down*
sich hinsetzen	*sit down*
sich rasieren	*shave*
sich Sorgen machen	*worry*
sich treffen	*meet*
sich verändern	*change*
sich etwas vorstellen	*imagine*

Aber:

sich amüsieren	*enjoy oneself*

Überprüfe hier, ob das Wissen sitzt

1 Setze die richtige Form des *self*-Pronomens in die Lücke ein.

a The cow hurt ________________ when it fell over.

b I ________________ would prefer to stay at home this weekend.

c The Greens never cook for ________________. They always eat out.

d Kevin, you'll have to leave the room if you can't behave ________________.

e Mrs Cobb didn't introduce ________________ to the class at all.

f We need help. We can't do this job ________________.

g Look, kids, if you can't do your homework ________________ , I'll help you.

2 Setze ein *self*-Pronomen oder ein Objektpronomen *(me, you, him, her, ...)* je nach Sinn des Satzes in die Lücken ein.

a In a test, always ask ________________ this question: "What does the examiner *(Prüfer)* expect ____________ to tell ____________?".

b We haven't time to show ________________ round now. I'm afraid you'll just have to look after ________________ until we get home.

c A lot of people buy material from a do-it-________________ store and then do the repairs ________________. This can save ________________ some money, but what about professional builders? It's really hard for ________________ when they don't have enough work.

d This problem isn't going to solve ________________ , is it? We have to sort ________________ out ________________.

e My husband Dennis is only interested in ________________. But what about ________________ and our children? He never thinks of ________________.

3 Setze die richtigen *Self*-Pronomen in die Sätze ein.

a Joe is teaching ________________ how to drive

b We all enjoyed ________________ at the party.

c I hurt ________________ when I was playing basketball.

d The Hoopers grow all their vegetables ________________.

e Did Kim repair her bike ________________?

f Come on, boys. Surely you can cook ________________ a meal!

1
a itself
b myself
c themselves
d yourself
e herself
f ourselves
g yourselves

2
a yourself – me – him
b you – yourselves
c yourself – themselves – them – them
d itself – it – ourselves
e himself – me – us

3
a Joe is teaching himself how to drive
b We all enjoyed ourselves at the party.
c I hurt myself when I was playing basketball.
d The Hoopers grow all their vegetables themselves.
e Did Kim repair her bike herself?
f Come on, boys. Surely you can cook yourselves a meal!

13

Die Pronomen *each other, one another*

Die beiden Pronomen *each other* und *one another* haben dieselbe Bedeutung und die gleiche Form für alle Personen.

Wollen wir eine wechselseitige Beziehung ausdrücken, benutzen wir *each other* oder *one another* statt eines *self*-Pronomens.
Life is much easier if people help ***each other.***
Das Leben ist viel leichter, wenn die Leute einander helfen.

The two drivers were shouting at ***one another.***
Die beiden Fahrer haben sich (gegenseitig) angeschrien.

Wenn du im Deutschen „einander" bzw. „miteinander" verwenden kannst, dann musst du im Englischen *each other* oder *one another* verwenden.

Überprüfe hier, ob das Wissen sitzt

1 Setze *each other* oder ein Reflexivpronomen in die Sätze ein.

a Cats spend a lot of time cleaning ________________.

b In our street everybody knows ________________.

c Children learn a lot by playing with ________________.

d Just go and look at ________________ in the mirror, Joe. Your face is dirty.

e Please do the test ________________, children.

f Of course identical twins look like ________________.

2 Vervollständige die Sätze mit *each other* bzw. einem Reflexivpronomen.

a Small schools are best because the pupils and teachers know ________________.

b Work in pairs and help ________________ to do the exercise.

c I'm sorry. You must ask the doctor ________________ , Hanna. He won't tell me anything.

d That funny man keeps talking to ________________.

e I always repair my bike ________________.

f The Smiths are shouting at ________________ again.

1 a Cats spend a lot of time cleaning themselves.
b In our street everybody knows each other.
c Children learn a lot by playing with each other.
d Just go and look at yourself in the mirror, Joe. Your face is dirty.
e Please do the test yourselves, children.
f Of course identical twins look like each other.

2 a … because the pupils and teachers know each other.
b Work in pairs and help each other to do the exercise.
c … ask the doctor yourself, Hanna. He won't tell me anything.
d That funny man keeps talking to himself.
e I always repair my bike myself.
f The Smiths are shouting at each other again.

14

Die Angaben *no/none, nobody/no one, nothing, nowhere*

Wir können die Mengenangabe *no* im Sinne von „kein/keiner" nur vor einem Nomen verwenden. Um eine Wiederholung von vorangegangenen Nomen zu vermeiden, verwenden wir *none*.
*We have **no bread** and **no milk** either.*
Wir haben kein Brot und auch keine Milch.

Sam: How much milk did you buy?
Sam: Wie viel Milch hast du gekauft?
*Joe: **None.***
Joe: Keine.

Wir verwenden *none* auch vor *of*-Fügungen.
***None of the boys** had done their homework.*
Keiner der Jungs hatte seine Hausaufgaben gemacht.

Die Zusammensetzungen von *no* sind *nothing, nobody/no one* und *nowhere*.
*Pam: Do you know **anything** about the accident?*
Pam: Weißt du irgendetwas über den Unfall?
*Jill: No, **nothing.***
Jill: Nein, nichts.

*There was **nobody/no one** in the room.*
Es war niemand im Zimmer.

*The child was **nowhere** in the park.*
Das Kind war nirgendwo im Park.

Überprüfe hier, ob das Wissen sitzt

Vervollständige die Sätze mit *no/none, nobody, nothing* oder *nowhere*.

a Annie fell off her bike, but ________________ stopped to help her.

b ________________ of our neighbours came to the barbecue.

c We can't go on holiday. We have ________________ money.

d Ask Joe. I'm afraid I know ________________ about computers.

e We went ________________. We stayed at home at the weekend.

a Annie fell off her bike, but nobody stopped to help her.
b None of our neighbours came to the barbecue.
c We can't go on holiday. We have no money.
d Ask Joe. I'm afraid I know nothing about computers.
e We went nowhere. We stayed at home at the weekend.

15

Each, every und seine Zusammensetzungen

Da im modernen Englisch *each* und *every* von der Bedeutung her fast identisch sind, kannst du die beiden Wörter beliebig verwenden – vorausgesetzt, dass sie unmittelbar vor einem Nomen stehen.
*Jane visits her grandparents **each/every weekend.***
Jane besucht ihre Großeltern jedes Wochenende.

***Each/every pupil** in the school has a laptop.*
Jeder Schüler in der Schule hat einen Laptop.

Es gibt aber Fälle, in denen wir nur *each* benutzen können, und zwar, wenn *each* die einzige Möglichkeit bei einer Auswahl von zweien ist.
Da wir *every* nur zusammen mit einem Nomen verwenden können, ist *each* die einzige Möglichkeit vor einer *of*-Fügung. Wenn das Wort allein – also ohne Nomen – steht, verwenden wir *each*.
***Each team** scored three goals.*
Jede Mannschaft erzielte drei Tore.

***Each of the children** had an ice-cream.*
Jedes Kind aß ein Eis.

*These T-shirts cost €20 **each.***
Diese T-Shirts kosten 20 € pro Stück.

Überprüfe hier, ob das Wissen sitzt

Verbinde einen Satzteil aus der linken Liste mit einem passenden aus der Liste rechts, um sinnvolle Sätze mit *each/every* zu bilden, z. B.:

Ted and Ben go to the youth club every day.

a	Ted and Ben go to the	at every meeting this year.
b	The teacher wants to speak	cost € 10 each.
c	The police stopped each of	did very well in the test.
d	We have two cakes and	each one tastes wonderful.
e	Every family I know is	worried about money at present.
f	Mr Gregg gave each of his	grandchildren a book.
g	We spend every New Year's Eve	on the North Sea coast.
h	The pizzas I bought	to each boy alone.
i	Each of the pupils in the class	the drivers for speeding.
j	We have discussed this problem	youth club every day.

b The teacher wants to speak to each boy alone.
c The police stopped each of the drivers for speeding.
d We have two cakes and each one tastes wonderful.
e Every family I know is worried about money at present.
f Mr Gregg gave each of his grandchildren a book.
g We spend every New Year's Eve on the North Sea coast.
h The pizzas I bought cost € 10 each.
i Each of the pupils in the class did very well in the test.
j We have discussed this problem at every meeting this year.

16

All (the) und *both*

■ *All (the)*

All ohne Artikel bedeutet „alle ohne Ausnahme aus einer unbegrenzten Zahl“. *All* mit Artikel heißt „alle ohne Ausnahme aus einer begrenzten Zahl“.

Ein häufiger Fehler ist das Weglassen des bestimmten Artikels bei einer begrenzten Zahl, weil wir im Deutschen in solchen Fällen keinen Artikel verwenden.

All cars *must stop.*
Alle Autos müssen anhalten.

All passengers *must have a ticket.*
Alle Passagiere müssen eine Fahrkarte haben.

All the boys *in the team played well.*
Alle Jungs in der Mannschaft spielten gut.

All the passengers *on the bus had a ticket.*
Alle Passagiere im Bus hatten eine Fahrkarte.

■ *Both*

Anders als bei dem deutschen Wort „beide“ kann das englische Wort *both* nie mit einem Artikel verwendet werden. Wollen wir „die beiden“ sagen, heißt es *the two.*

Both drivers *were going much too fast.*
Beide Fahrer fuhren viel zu schnell.

Both boys *missed the Maths test.*
Beide Jungs haben die Mathearbeit verpasst.

Are ***the two girls*** *in your class?*
Sind die beiden Mädchen in deiner Klasse?

The two boys missed *the Maths test.*
Die beiden Jungs haben die Mathearbeit verpasst.

Überprüfe hier, ob das Wissen sitzt

Vervollständige die Sätze mit *each* bzw. *every* oder *all (the)* bzw. *both*.

a Do these CDs only cost $2 ______________ ?

b ______________ French people we met on holiday were very friendly.

c ______________ passengers must have a ticket before getting on to the bus.

d In tennis, ______________ players have a tennis racket.

e The police arrested two men. They said that ______________ of them were drunk.

f In this game ______________ person needs seven cards.

g The two cars in the accident were ______________ Rovers.

h We take our dog for a long walk ______________ day.

a Do these CDs only cost $2 **each**?
b **All the** French people we met on holiday were very friendly.
c **All** passengers must have a ticket before getting on to the bus.
d In tennis, **both** players have a tennis racket.
e The police arrested two men. They said that **both** of them were drunk.
f In this game **each** person needs seven cards.
g The two cars in the accident were **both** Rovers.
h We take our dog for a long walk **every** day.

17

Was ist ein Adjektiv?

Adjektive beschreiben Menschen, Tiere, Sachen und Ereignisse. Genau wie im Deutschen stehen Adjektive entweder unmittelbar vor dem betroffenen Nomen oder unmittelbar nach *be*.

Tiger is a ***nice cat.***
Tiger ist eine nette Katze.

Cathy has bought a ***new pullover.***
Cathy hat einen neuen Pulli gekauft.

I saw a ***bad accident*** *today.*
Heute sah ich einen schlimmen Unfall.

The test ***wasn't difficult.***
Der Test war nicht schwierig.

These apples ***taste wonderful.***
Diese Äpfel schmecken wunderbar.

Es gibt einige Verben der sinnlichen Wahrnehmung, die wie Nomen von Adjektiven näher bestimmt werden.
Am wichtigsten sind:

look	aussehen	*Mum looks tired.*	Mama sieht müde aus.
smell	duften, riechen	*The cake smells good.*	Der Kuchen duftet gut.
sound	klingen	*Tiger sounds frightened.*	Tiger klingt ängstlich.
taste	schmecken	*The fish tasts awful.*	Der Fisch schmeckt schrecklich.

Überprüfe hier, ob das Wissen sitzt

1 Sieh dir den Text an und unterstreiche die Adjektive.

Have you seen my new room? It's great. Dad made me a fantastic desk, and mum got me a lovely chair from the new shop in town. Oh, and I've got my big brother's old bed, too. It's very soft and comfortable. There's only one problem. We painted the walls yesterday. They look fine, but the room smells awful *(furchtbar)* at the moment.

2 Übersetze.

a Der neue Nachbar ist freundlich.

____

b Er trägt immer einen schwarzen Mantel und einen alten Hut, selbst an warmen Sommertagen.

____

____

c Mit seinem runden Kopf, den kleinen Ohren und der dicken Brille sieht er wie eine Eule aus.

____

____

1 Have you seen my **new** room? It's **great**. Dad made me a **fantastic** desk, and mum got me a **lovely** chair from the **new** shop in town. Oh, and I've got my **big** brother's **old** bed, too. It's very **soft** and **comfortable**. There's only one problem. We painted the walls yesterday. They look **fine**, but the room smells **awful** at the moment.

2 a The new neighbour is friendly.
b He always wears a black coat and an old hat, even on warm summer days.
c With his round head, little ears and thick glasses he looks like an owl.

18

Die Steigerung von Adjektiven

Im Englischen gibt es zwei Steigerungen, eine auf *-er/-est* und eine mit *more/most*.

Mit *-er/-est* werden die folgenden Arten von Adjektiven gesteigert:

- alle einsilbigen Adjektive, z. B.:

big	*bigger*	*biggest*
clean	*cleaner*	*cleanest*
fast	*faster*	*fastest*
loud	*louder*	*loudest*
nice	*nicer*	*nicest*
old	*older*	*oldest*

- alle zweisilbigen Adjektive, die auf *-y* enden; beim Anhängen von *-er/est* wird das *-y* zum *-i*, z. B.:

angry	*angrier*	*angriest*	wütend, verärgert
early	*earlier*	*earliest*	früh
happy	*happier*	*happiest*	froh
hungry	*hungrier*	*hungriest*	hungrig
pretty	*prettier*	*prettiest*	hübsch
silly	*sillier*	*silliest*	dumm

Cathy: Bonzo is really ***fast,*** *isn't he?*
Cathy: Bonzo ist echt schnell, nicht?

Tom: What? Lucky is ***faster.*** *He is* ***the fastest dog*** *in the park.*
Tom: Was? Lucky ist schneller. Er ist der schnellste Hund im Park.

Kevin is ***the silliest boy*** *in our street.*
Kevin ist der albernste Junge in unserer Straße.

Wir gebrauchen more/most mit ...

- ... zweisilbigen Adjektiven, die nicht auf -y enden, z.B.:

boring	*more boring*	*most boring*	langweilig
careful	*more careful*	*most careful*	vorsichtig
famous	*more famous*	*most famous*	berühmt
helpful	*more helpful*	*most helpful*	hilfsbereit
nervous	*more nervous*	*most nervous*	nervös

- ... allen Adjektiven mit mehr als zwei Silben, z.B.:

beautiful	*more beautiful*	*most beautiful*	schön
dangerous	*more dangerous*	*most dangerous*	gefährlich
difficult	*more difficult*	*most difficult*	schwierig
exciting	*more exciting*	*most exciting*	spannend
expensive	*more expensive*	*most expensive*	teuer
interesting	*more interesting*	*most interesting*	interessant

Diese Adjektive werden unregelmäßig gesteigert:

bad	*worse*	*worst*	schlecht
good	*better*	*best*	gut
much	*more*	*most*	viel
far	*farther/further*	*farthest/furthest*	weit

Tim: That was ***the most difficult*** *test I've ever done.*
Tim: Das war der schwierigste Test, den ich je gemacht habe.
Sue: Really? I found the last test ***more difficult.***
Sue: Wirklich? Ich fand den letzten Test schwieriger.

Cathy is ***good,*** *but Elli is* ***better.*** *She's the* ***best*** *girl in the class.*
Cathy ist gut, aber Elli ist besser. Sie ist das beste Mädchen in der Klasse.

Überprüfe hier, ob das Wissen sitzt

1 Vervollständige die Tabelle mit den Steigerungsformen der vorgegebenen Adjektive.

Adjektiv	Komparativ	Superlativ
bad		
beautiful	*more beautiful*	*most beautiful*
careful		
cheap	*cheaper*	*cheapest*
easy		
good		
interesting		
large		
lovely		
many		

2 Setze die Komparativ- oder Superlativform der Adjektive in Klammern in die Sätze ein.

a Sam and Eric are twins *(Zwillinge)*, but Sam is the ________________ (big) of the two.

Yes, but Eric is the ________________ (clever).

b Who is the ________________ (kind) teacher here?

Miss Jones. She is the ________________ (nice) teacher I know.

c I don't like Dirk. He's the ________________ (noisy) boy I know. And the ________________ (silly), too.

Oh, come on. I know lots of ________________ (bad) boys.

d Can I have ________________ (many) chips, please?

No. You've had the ________________ (many) already.

e What's ________________ (interesting), TV or reading?

Well, TV can be OK, but a good book is ________________ (exciting), I think.

f I got a ________________ (good) mark *(Note)* in maths today than last time.

So what? That was the ________________ (easy) test we've ever had. Last week's test was ________________ (difficult).

3 Ergänze die fehlenden Formen.

bad	*worse*	*worst*	schlecht
			weit
			viel
			einige
			wenig(e)

1 bad – worse – worst; careful – more careful – most careful
easy – easier – easiest; good – better – best
interesting – more interesting – most interesting
large – larger – largest; lovely – lovelier – loveliest; many – more – most

2 a bigger – cleverer
b kindest – nicest
c noisiest – the silliest – worse
d more – most
e more interesting – more exciting
f better – easiest – more difficult

3 far – further – furthest – *weit;*
much – more – most – *viel;*
some – more – most – *einige;*
a few, few – less – least – *wenig(e)*

19

Adverbien der Art und Weise

Wir benutzen Adverbien, um Verben näher zu beschreiben.
Ein Adverb sagt also, **wie** jemand irgendeine Tätigkeit ausführt.

Hat das Verb kein Objekt, steht das Adverb unmittelbar nach dem Verb.
Hat aber das Verb ein Objekt, dann steht das Adverb unmittelbar vor dem Verb.
Tipp: Im Englischen ist ein Verb + Objekt wie ein verliebtes Paar – nichts darf dazwischen!
*The red car was going **slowly.***
Das rote Auto fuhr langsam.

*The blue car was going **fast.***
Das blaue Auto fuhr schnell.

*The blue car **easily** won the race.*
Das blaue Auto hat das Rennen leicht gewonnen.

*Frank behaved **terribly** at school today.*
Frank benahm sich heute fürchterlich in der Schule.

Adverbien bilden wir mit wenigen Ausnahmen, indem wir an das entsprechende Adjektiv ein *-ly* anfügen:

Adjektiv	Adverb	
careful	*carefully*	vorsichtig
dangerous	*dangerously*	gefährlich
quick	*quickly*	schnell
slow	*slowly*	langsam

Beachte diese Schreibregeln beim Anhängen von *-ly:*
Bei Adjektiven, die auf *-y* enden, wird das *-y* zum *-i,* z.B.:

angry	*angrily*	verärgert
easy	*easily*	einfach
lucky	*luckily*	zum Glück
pretty	*prettily*	hübsch

Endet das Adjektiv auf *-le,* entfällt das *-le* (das *-ly* wird angehängt), z.B.:

possible	*possibly*	wahrscheinlich
probable	*probably*	möglich
simple	*simply*	einfach
terrible	*terribly*	fürchterlich

Diese Adjektive haben als Adverb eine unregelmäßige Form:

Adjektiv	Adverb	
fast	*fast*	schnell
good	*well*	gut
hard	*hard*	schwierig, hart
high	*high*	hoch

Überprüfe hier, ob das Wissen sitzt

1 Bilde Adverbien von diesen Adjektiven:

slow ______________	angry ______________
hungry ______________	careful ______________
sad ______________	kind ______________
lucky ______________	noisy ______________
wonderful ______________	merry ______________

2 Suche dir ein passendes Adjektiv, bilde davon das Adverb und setze es dann ein.

bad – beautiful – careful – good – easy – quiet – slow – happy – quick

a The children went on holiday happily. No more school!

b Adam drank the lemonade ______________. He was thirsty.

c Amy did her homework ______________. She is a good pupil.

d Bob walked home ______________. It took him nearly an hour.

e Kirsty listened to her CDs ______________. Mrs Nunn was asleep.

f Amy plays the piano ______________. She will ______________ win the competition *(Wettbewerb)*.

g Oh dear, Bob sang the song ______________. I don't think he can sing very ______________.

3 Entscheide, ob du ein Adjektiv oder ein Adverb benötigst.

a (sad) "Why are you so ______________, Amy?"
"I've lost Spooky," said Amy ______________.

b (kind) Because Tom was a ______________ boy, he said ______________ : "Well, I'll help you to find your dog."

c (quiet) "Bob, be ______________ , please. Play your CDs ______________ or go outside."

d (angry) Mr Carter is ______________ . "Stand up, Bob," he said ______________ .

e (hungry) "Here comes Adam. He looks ______________ ," said Mrs Cobb. "Hello, Mrs Cobb. That cake smells good," said Adam ______________ .

f (quiet) Amy spoke very ______________ in class today and Miss Jones couldn't hear her. "Don't talk so ______________ ," she said. "I can't understand you."

g (good) Amy works ______________ at school. She is a ______________ pupil.

1

slowly	angrily
hungrily	carefully
sadly	kindly
luckily	noisily
wonderfully	merrily

2
a (The children went on holiday happily.)
b Adam drank the lemonade quickly.
c Amy did her homework carefully
d Bob walked home slowly.
e Kirsty listened to her CDs quietly.
f Amy plays the piano beautifully. She will easily win the competition.
g Oh dear, Bob sang the song badly. I don't think he can sing very well.

3
a sad – sadly
b kind – kindly
c quiet – quietly
d angry – angrily
e hungry – hungrily
f quietly – quietly
g well – good

20

Die Steigerung von Adverbien

Adverbien auf *-ly* steigern wir mit *more/most.*
*Mary dances **more beautifully** than Tom.*
Mary tanzt schöner als Tom.

Adverbien, die die gleiche Form wie das Adjektiv haben, steigern wir mit *-er/-est.*
*Lucky can run **faster than** Bonzo.*
Lucky kann schneller laufen als Bonzo.

Die Adverbien *well* und *badly* sind unregelmäßig:

well	*better*	*best*	gut
bad	*worse*	*worst*	schlecht

*Frank sings **worse than** me.*
Frank singt schlechter als ich.

Überprüfe hier, ob das Wissen sitzt

Setze die richtige Form des gesteigerten Adverbs ein.

a I work ____________ (happily) when the sun is shining than when it's raining.

b Miss Jones drives ____________ (carefully) than Mr Carter.

c You always work ____________ (well) than most but today you did ____________ (well).

d Tom can run ____________ (fast) than Adam.

e Can't you play your music ____________ (quietly) than you usually do?

f The school team played ____________ (badly) than they did last week.

g Kirsty worked ____________ (hard) than the other pupils and got the best mark.

h Tom jumped ____________ (high) than Bob but Kirsty jumped 2 cm ____________ (high). She jumped the ____________ (high) in the form.

a I work more happily when the sun is shining than when it's raining.
b Miss Jones drives more carefully than Mr Carter.
c You always work better than most but today you did best.
d Tom can run faster than Adam.
e Can't you play your music more quietly than you usually do?
f The school team played worse than they did last week.
g Kirsty worked harder than the other pupils and got the best mark.
h Tom jumped higher than Bob but Kirsty jumped 2 cm higher. She jumped the highest in the form.

21

Vergleichssätze

Adjektive

Wir vergleichen Tiere, Personen usw. in Sätzen wie folgt:

kein Unterschied	*as fast ... as*	so schnell ... wie
positiver Unterschied	*taller ...than*	größer ... als
negativer Unterschied	*not as tall ... as*	nicht so groß ... wie

*Bonzo is **as fast as** Lucky.*
Bonzo ist so schnell wie Lucky.

*Tim is **taller than** Cathy.*
Tim ist größer als Cathy.

*Cathy is **not as tall as** her brother.*
Cathy ist nicht so groß wie ihr Bruder.

Adverbien

Wollen wir die Tätigkeiten von Tieren, Personen usw. in Sätzen vergleichen, haben wir folgende Möglichkeiten:

as ... as	genauso ... wie
not as ... as	nicht so ... wie
more/less ... than	mehr/weniger ... als

*Bonzo runs **as fast as** Lucky.*
Bonzo rennt so schnell wie Lucky.

*Tim does **not** work **as hard as** Cathy.*
Tim arbeitet nicht so hart wie Cathy.

*Women drive **more safely** than men.*
Frauen fahren sicherer als Männer.

*Cathy speaks German **less well** than Elli.*
Cathy spricht weniger gut Deutsch als Elli.

Überprüfe hier, ob das Wissen sitzt

1 Stelle Vergleiche in Sätzen her. Verwende die Adjektive aus den Klammern. Schreibe auf ein extra Blatt.

a Hamburg has about 1.7 million inhabitants *(Bewohner)*, and Munich has around 1.4. (small)

b Ben's flat is 65 square metres and so is ours. (big)

c There are three kids in my family. I'm fifteen, my brother Tony is ten and my sister Madison is twelve. (young)

2 Bei einem Autorennen fahren die Wagen in dieser Reihenfolge:

1 – 7 ⟨ 2 / 5 ⟩ 8 ⟨ 3 / 6 ⟩ 4.

Nummer 1 ist der schnellste Wagen; Nummer 4 der langsamste. Neben Nummer 2 fährt der Wagen 5; auf gleicher Höhe wie Nummer 3 ist Wagen 6.
Bilde Vergleichssätze mit *than* und *as ... as* und *not as ... as*.

a 6 *is not driving as fast* ______ as 8.

b 3 ______ as 6.

c 1 ______ 7.

d 2 ______ 5.

e 4 ______ 3.

f 7 ______ 2.

1 a Munich is smaller than Hamburg.
b Our flat is as big as Ben's.
c Tony is two years younger than Madison. Tony is the youngest child in the family.

2 a 6 is not driving as fast as 8.
b 3 is driving as fast as 6.
c 1 is driving faster than 7.
d 2 is driving as fast as 5.
e 4 is not driving as fast as 3.
f 7 is driving faster than 2.

Verschiedene Arten von Adverbien und ihre Stellung

Satzadverbien

Satzadverbien – wie *fortunately/unfortunately* (leider), *in fact* (in der Tat), *luckily* (glücklicherweise)/*unluckily, maybe* (vielleicht), *naturally* (natürlich), *obviously* (offensichtlich), *of course* (selbstverständlich) und *perhaps* (vielleicht) – bestimmen einen ganzen Satz. Daher stehen sie am Satzanfang.

***Luckily** the rain soon stopped.*
Glücklicherweise hörte der Regen bald auf.

***Maybe** we can find a taxi.*
Vielleicht können wir ein Taxi finden.

Adverbien der Art und Weise

Adverbien der Art und Weise (Hilfsfrage: Wie?) – z. B. *badly, beautifully, politely* (höflich), *quickly* usw. – stehen in der Regel am Satzende.

*The car was going too **quickly**.*
Das Auto fuhr zu schnell.

*The man spoke to us **politely**.*
Der Mann sprach höflich zu uns.

Zeit- und Ortsadverbien

Zeitadverbien (Hilfsfrage: Wann?) und Ortsadverbien (Hilfsfragen: Wo?, Wohin?) stehen in der Regel am Satzende.

*Helen went home **at 3 o'clock**.*
Helen ging um 3 Uhr nach Hause.

*Tom lives **in London**.*
Tom lebt in London.

Stehen ein Zeitadverb und ein Ortsadverb zusammen am Satzende, dann gilt die Reihenfolge Ort vor Zeit (O vor Z):

*Our plane leaves **New York at 10.30**.*
Unser Flugzeug verlässt New York um 10.30 Uhr.

Eine Anreihung von Orts- bzw. Zeitadverbien am Satzende wird vom Spezifischen zum Allgemeinen geordnet:
*Our plane lands **at 10.30 on 10 May.***
Unser Flugzeug landet um 10.30 Uhr am 10. Mai.

*They live **in a flat in Church Lane in York.***
Sie leben in einer Wohnung in der Church Lane in York.

Kommt ein Adverb der Art und Weise dazu, ist die Reihenfolge Art und Weise – Ort – Zeit (Manner – Place – Time):
*Mary sang **beautifully at the concert last night.***
Mary sang schön bei dem Konzert letzte Nacht.

Häufigkeitsadverbien

Besteht ein Häufigkeitsadverb aus einem Wort wie *always, never, often,* steht es unmittelbar vor dem Vollverb bzw. nach einer Form von *be.*
*Helen **always** walks to the office.*
Helen läuft immer zum Büro.

*Tom is **sometimes** late for work.*
Tom kommt manchmal spät zur Arbeit.

Besteht das Adverb aus mehr als einem Wort, steht es am Satzende.
*We go shopping **every Saturday.***
Wir gehen jeden Samstag einkaufen.

Gradadverbien

Gradadverbien – z.B. *a bit* (ein bisschen), *absolutely, completely* (völlig), *hardly* (kaum), *nearly* (fast), *rather* (ziemlich), *really* (eigentlich, wirklich), *totally, wholly* (gänzlich) – haben die gleiche Position wie Adjektive. Sie stehen unmittelbar vor dem Wort, das sie beschreiben.
*The baby **nearly** died.*
Das Baby starb fast.

*Are you **completely** certain?*
Bist du völlig sicher?

*The film was **quite** good.*
Der Film war ganz gut.

Überprüfe hier, ob das Wissen sitzt

1 Welche Position im Satz gilt für die angegebenen Adverbien? Kreuze die richtige Spalte an.

Adverb	Satzanfang	Satzmitte	Satzende
now and then			
of course			
in Berlin			
at 7 o'clock			
every day			
often			
completely			
sometimes			
beautifully			
unfortunately			
rather			
at home			

2 Stelle die Adverbien an die richtige Position im Satz wie im Beispiel a.

a Harry goes + to school/every morning/at 8 o'clock.

Harry goes to school at 8 o'clock every morning.

b My father was born + 1985/on 6 April/at midnight

____

c Betty has breakfast + before going to work/never

____

d Our Biology teacher shouted at us + in class/very rudely/today

____

e I missed my bus + this morning, unfortunately

____

f Janna is unhappy + rather, at the moment, of course

____

g Ben understands German, but he can't speak it + very fluently/quite well

____

h I'll meet you + tomorrow afternoon/outside the town hall/at 4 o'clock

____

1

Adverb	Satzanfang	Satzmitte	Satzende
now and then			x
of course	x		
in Berlin			x
at 7 o'clock			x
every day			x
often		x	
completely		x	
sometimes		x	
beautifully			x
unfortunately	x		
rather		x	
at home			x

2
b My father was born at midnight on 6 April 1985.
c Betty never has breakfast before going to work.
d Our Biology teacher shouted at us very rudely in class today.
e Unfortunately I missed my bus this morning.
f Of course Janna is rather unhappy at the moment.
g Ben understands German quite well, but he can't speak it very fluently.
h I'll meet you outside the town hall at 4 o'clock tomorrow afternoon.

23

some, any und ihre Zusammensetzungen

Wenn wir über eine unbestimmte Menge reden wollen, benutzen wir *some* oder *any* (einige/etwas). Diese beiden Wörter haben genau dieselbe Bedeutung, werden aber unterschiedlich benutzt.
Wir gebrauchen *some* in bejahten Aussagen und *any* in verneinten Aussagen und Fragen.
I bought ***some potatoes*** *today.*
Ich habe heute einige Kartoffeln gekauft.

I didn't buy ***any apples.***
Ich habe keine Äpfel gekauft.

Did you buy ***any tomatoes?***
Hast du Tomaten gekauft?

Ist jedoch eine Frage eigentlich eine höfliche Bitte oder ein höfliches Angebot, benutzen wir ebenfalls *some.*
May I have ***some sugar,*** *please?*
Darf ich etwas Zucker haben, bitte?

Would you like ***some chips,*** *Cathy?*
Hättest du gerne Pommes frites, Cathy?

Wir benutzen die Zusammensetzungen von *some* und *any* – also *somebody/anybody, someone/anyone, something/anything, somewhere/anywhere* – in genau derselben Art und Weise.
Jill: There's ***somebody*** *in the garden.*
Tom: I can't see ***anybody.***
Jill: Es ist jemand im Garten
Tom: Ich kann niemanden sehen.

Tiger is ***somewhere*** *here, but I can't see her* ***anywhere.***
Tiger ist irgendwo hier, aber ich kann sie nirgendwo sehen.

Bob: Do you know ***anything*** *about animals?*
Bill: I know ***something*** *about them.*
Bob: Weißt du irgendetwas über Tiere?
Bill: Ich weiß ein bisschen darüber.

Überprüfe hier, ob das Wissen sitzt

Setze *some*, *any* oder eine ihrer Zusammensetzungen in die Sätze ein.

a I haven't got ________ lemonade, but I can give you ________ cold milk.

b Miss Jones can't find her purse ________, but it must be ________ in the classroom. Or do you think that ________ has taken it?

c Adam's so lazy. He never does ________ work.

d – Have you got ________ money?
– Well, I've got ________ at home.

e Can ________ here speak German?

f Amy can give you ________ books to read. Bob hasn't got ________ books at all.

g There's ________ wrong with our car. Can you do ________ about it?

a I haven't got any lemonade, but I can give you some cold milk.
b Miss Jones can't find her purse anywhere, but it must be somewhere in the classroom. Or do you think that somebody has taken it?
c Adam's so lazy. He never does any work.
d – Have you got any money?
– Well, I've got some at home.
e Can anybody here speak German?
f Amy can give you some books to read. Bob hasn't got any books at all.
g There's something wrong with our car. Can you do anything about it?

much/many/a lot of, plenty of – (a) few, (a) little

much/many/a lot of, plenty of

Wir gebrauchen *many* mit zählbaren Nomen und *much* mit nichtzählbaren Nomen in verneinten Aussagen und Fragen.

We don't have ***many rolls.***
Wir haben nicht viele Brötchen.

We don't eat ***much meat.***
Wir essen nicht viel Fleisch.

Why did you buy so ***much bread?***
Warum hast du so viel Brot gekauft?

In bejahten Aussagen benutzen wir *a lot of* mit zählbaren sowie nichtzählbaren Nomen. Häufig können wir *much* bzw. *many* durch *a lot of* ersetzen, nicht aber nach *as, so, too, how* und *very*. Wollen wir „mehr als genug" ausdrücken, ersetzen wir *a lot of* durch *plenty of*.

We have ***a lot of apples*** *and a* ***lot of oranges,*** *too.*
Wir haben viele Äpfel und auch viele Orangen.

Don't eat ***so much cake.*** *There's* ***too much sugar*** *in it.*
Iss nicht so viel Kuchen. Es ist zu viel Zucker darin.

We have ***plenty of bread*** *and rolls, too.*
Wir haben massenweise Brot und auch Brötchen.

(a) few, (a) little

Wir gebrauchen *a little* (ein wenig) und *little* (wenig) mit nichtzählbaren und *a few* (ein paar) und *few* (wenige) mit zählbaren Nomen. Diese Regel gilt für alle Satzarten, also für bejahte und verneinte Aussagen und Fragen.

Would you like a ***little bread*** *with your soup?*
Hättest du gerne ein bisschen Brot zu deiner Suppe?

Can I have ***a few chips,*** *please?*
Kann ich ein paar Pommes frites haben, bitte?

Few players *in the team are as good as Tim.*
Wenige Spieler in der Mannschaft sind so gut wie Tim.

Überprüfe hier, ob das Wissen sitzt

Vervollständige die Sätze.

a There is only ______________ beer in the glass. *(wenig)*

b Julia has got ______________ flowers in her basket. *(viel)*

c The bus has not got ______________ passengers in it. *(viele)*

d Mrs Drew hasn't got ______________ money left. *(viel)*

e The milk bottle hasn't got ______________ milk in it. *(viel)*

f This teacher has got ______________ work to do. *(viel)*

g There aren't __________ minutes to go before the new year. *(viele)*

h There are only ______________ toffees left. *(wenige)*

a There is only a little beer in the glass.
b Julia has got a lot of flowers in her basket.
c The bus has not got many passengers in it.
d Mrs Drew hasn't got much money left.
e The milk bottle hasn't got much milk in it.
f This teacher has got a lot of work to do.
g There aren't many minutes to go before the new year.
h There are only a few toffees left.

Präpositionen des Ortes und der Zeit

Wir benutzen Präpositionen, um eine Beziehung auszudrücken. Im ersten Beispiel unten wird die Beziehung zwischen der Maus und dem Tisch gezeigt. Am besten lernt man Präpositionen immer als Teil einer Redewendung.

The mouse sat ***on the table.***
Die Maus saß auf dem Tisch.

I live ***in Bristol.***
Ich wohne in Bristol.

The concert begins ***at 8 pm.***
Das Konzert beginnt um 20 Uhr.

Präpositionen des Ortes

at the station	am Bahnhof
at the baker's	beim Bäcker
at the chemist's	in der Apotheke
at the supermarket	im Supermarkt
at home	zu Hause
at school	in der Schule
at 12 Albert Street	in der Albert Street 12
at work	bei der Arbeit
at the seaside	am Meer
at Kate's party	auf Kates Party
at the table	am Tisch
at the top/bottom	oben/unten
in the street	auf der Straße
in the sky	am Himmel
in the country	auf dem Land
in the middle	in der Mitte
in the photo	auf dem Foto
in the world	auf der Welt
in town	in der Stadt
in the car	im Auto

on the road	auf der Straße
on the board	an der Tafel
on the wall	an der Wand
on the beach	am Strand
on the bus/train/...	im Bus/Zug/...
on the way to	unterwegs nach
on the left/right	links/rechts

Präpositionen der Zeit

at Christmas	zu Weihnachten
at 4 o'clock	um 4 Uhr
at breakfast/lunch/...	beim Frühstück/beim Mittagessen/...
at night	bei Nacht
at the weekend/at weekends	am Wochenende
at the moment	im Augenblick
at present	zur Zeit
at once	sofort
in time	rechtzeitig
in the morning/afternoon/...	am Morgen/Nachmittag
in a minute	gleich
in summer/winter/...	im Sommer/Winter/...
on my birthday	an meinem Geburtstag
on time	pünktlich

Beachte: Anders als im Deutschen werden im Englischen *last* und *next* ohne Präposition verwendet:

I saw Cathy Bell ***last weekend.***
Ich sah Cathy Bell am letzten Wochenende.

We are going ***to Austria*** *next winter.*
Wir fahren im nächsten Winter nach Österreich.

Überprüfe hier, ob das Wissen sitzt

1 Übersetze und benutze dabei diese Präpositionen des Ortes:

above	*über*	near	*nah*
at	*an*	next to	*neben*
behind	*hinter*	on	*auf*
between	*zwischen*	outside	*draußen*
in front of	*vor*	round	*rund (um)*
inside	*in*	under	*unter*

a neben dem Baum ______________________________

b auf dem Dach ______________________________

c draußen ______________________________

d hinter dem Baum ______________________________

e um den Baum herum ______________________________

f vor dem Baum ______________________________

g in der Nähe des Hauses ______________________________

h unter dem Tisch ______________________________

i auf dem Tisch ______________________________

j über dem Dach ______________________________

k in dem Topf ______________________________

l zwischen den Bäumen ______________________________

2 Trage *in, at* oder *on* ein.

a Spooky was born ______ 1997.

b He was born ______ 6th June.

c He eats a lot ______ the morning, but he doesn't eat anything ______ night.

d He goes to the park with Amy ______ the weekends.

e He's looking for Easter eggs ______ Easter and gets a big sausage ______ Christmas.

f He likes the snow ______ winter and he likes swimming ______ the summer.

g He always waits for the children ______ the afternoon.

h ______ Sundays Spooky and the whole family go to the park.

1
a next to the tree
b on the roof
c outside
d behind the tree
e round the tree
f in front of the tree
g near the house
h under the table
i at the table
j above the roof
k in/inside the pot
l between the trees

2
a Spooky was born in 1997.
b He was born on 6th June.
c He eats a lot in the morning, but he doesn't eat anything at night.
d He goes to the park with Amy at the weekends.
e He's looking for Easter eggs at Easter and gets a big sausage at Christmas.
f He likes the snow in winter and he likes swimming in the summer.
g He always waits for the children in the afternoon.
h On Sundays Spooky and the whole family go to the park.

26

Die häufigsten Konjunktionen

Wir benutzen Konjunktionen (Bindewörter), um Wörter, Satzglieder oder Sätze miteinander zu verbinden.

*Mrs Bell likes TV **and** reading.*
Mrs Bell mag fernsehen und lesen.

*You can walk **or** go by bus.*
Du kannst laufen oder mit dem Bus fahren.

*Elli tried on the trousers, **but** they were too big.*
Elli probierte die Hose an, aber sie war zu groß.

*Tiger was sleeping **when** I saw her.*
Tiger schlief gerade, als ich sie sah.

*Frank can't come **because** he's ill.*
Frank kann nicht kommen, weil er krank ist.

*We lost the game **although/though** we trained hard.*
Wir haben das Spiel verloren, obwohl wir hart trainiert haben.

Die häufigsten Konjunktionen sind:

although/though	obwohl
and	und
as soon as	sobald
because	weil
because of	wegen
but	aber
or	oder
when	zwei Bedeutungen: „als" oder „wenn"

Überprüfe hier, ob das Wissen sitzt

Verbinde die Satzglieder und Sätze sinnvoll mit einer Konjunktion.

a We will still go to the zoo ______________ the weather is bad.

b Some people are rich ______________ they still want more money.

c Mr Carter was angry ______________ Bob was late.

d The boys ______________ girls walk to school.

e You can fly to New York ______________ you can go by boat.

f Mr Parker is still reading ______________ it's very late.

g The sun was shining all the time ______________ I was in London.

h We will leave ______________ you arrive.

i Everybody started shouting ______________ the concert began.

j Spooky ______________ Coco wanted some more sausage.

k Does Tom have a sister ______________ a brother?

l I will show you my dad's new web cam ________________ he has got it.

a We will still go to the zoo although/though the weather is bad.
b Some people are rich, but they still want more money.
c Mr Carter was angry because Bob was late.
d The boys and girls walk to school.
e You can fly to New York and/or you can go by boat.
f Mr Parker is still reading although/though it's very late.
g The sun was shining all the time when I was in London.
h We will leave when/as soon as you arrive.
i Everybody started shouting when/as soon as the concert began.
j Spooky and Coco wanted some more sausage.
k Does Tom have a sister or a brother?
l I will show you my dad's new web cam as soon as/when he has got it.

27

Angaben der Zeit

Für alle Zeiten von Mitternacht bis 12 Uhr mittags benutzen wir die Buchstaben *a.m.* Für alle Zeiten von 12 Uhr mittags bis Mitternacht benutzen wir *p.m.:*

*It's **9 a.m.***

Es ist 9 Uhr (vormittags).

*The film starts at **7 p.m.***

Der Film beginnt um 19 Uhr.

Bei vollen Stunden können wir *o'clock (= of the clock)* benutzen. Dann entfällt *a.m./p.m.:*

*It's **9 o'clock.***

Es ist 9 Uhr.

*The film starts at **7 o'clock.***

Der Film beginnt um 7 Uhr.

Bei den viertelstündigen Schritten sagen wir *(a) quarter past, half past* und *(a) quarter to* ohne *a.m./p.m.*

***It's (a) quarter** past three.*

Es ist Viertel nach drei.

It's half past ten.

Es ist halb elf.

***It's (a) quarter** to elven.*

Es ist Viertel vor elf.

Die fünfminütigen Schritte werden meist ohne das Wort *minutes* ausgedrückt, also *ten past three, twenty-five past seven, twenty to ten, five to eleven.*

Bei einminütigen Zeiten müssen wir das Wort *minutes* hinzufügen, also *seven minutes past five, eighteen minutes to nine.*

Merke dir diese wichtigen Wendungen:

What time is it? *What's the time?*	Wie spät ist es?
at 10 o'clock	um 10 Uhr
at about 5 o'clock	gegen 5 Uhr

Tipp:
Findest du die englischen Uhrzeiten ziemlich kompliziert? Nur keine Bange! Im Englischen können wir die Zeiten nur mit Zahlen, also digital, sagen:
It's two fifteen.
Es ist zwei Uhr fünfzehn.

Our break is from ***eleven thirty to eleven forty-five.***
Unsere Pause ist von elf Uhr dreißig bis elf Uhr fünfundvierzig.

Überprüfe hier, ob das Wissen sitzt

1 Sieh dir die Abfahrtszeiten an und vervollständige die Sätze unten. Verwende *past* und *to*.

Trains from Norwich Thorpe	
07.10	Sheringham
08.05	Great Yarmouth
09.00	London (Liverpool Street)
10.45	Cambridge
14.45	Cromer
16.30	Ipswich
17.22	King's Lynn

The train to ...

a ... Sheringham leaves Norwich at *ten past seven* ________ a.m.

b ... Great Yarmouth goes at ________ a.m.

c ... London leaves at ________ a.m.

d ... Cambridge is at ________ a.m.

e ... Cromer goes ________ p.m.

f ... Ipswich ________ p.m.

g ... King's Lynn ________ p.m.

TESTEN • TESTEN • TESTEN • TESTEN • TESTEN • TESTEN • TESTEN

2 a Für welche Zeiten stehen die Buchstaben *a.m.?*

____

b Für welche Zeiten stehen die Buchstaben *p.m.?*

____

c Wann entfallen *a.m.* und *p.m.?*

____

3 Übersetze die Uhrzeiten.

a 7 Uhr ______________________________

b 8.25 Uhr ______________________________

c 9.35 Uhr ______________________________

d Fünf Minuten vor neun ________________________

e 4.30 Uhr ______________________________

f Viertel vor Zwei ___________________________

g Zwanzig vor Vier ___________________________

h Viertel nach 11 ____________________________

1 a (... Sheringham leaves Norwich at ten past seven a.m.)
b ... Great Yarmouth goes at five (minutes) past eight a.m.
c ... London leaves at nine o'clock a.m.
d ... Cambridge is at (a) quarter to eleven/ten forty-five a.m.
e ... Cromer goes (a) quarter to three/two forty-five p.m.
f ... Ipswich half (past) four/four thirty p.m.
g ... King's Lynn twenty-two minutes past five/five twenty-two p.m.

2 Siehe Seite 84.

3 a seven o'clock
b twenty-five (minutes) past eight/eight twenty-five
c twenty-five (minutes) to ten/nine thirty-five
d five (minutes) to nine/eight fifty-five
e half (past) four/four thirty
f (a) quarter to two/one forty-five
g twenty (minutes) to four/three forty
g (a) quarter past eleven/eleven fifteen

Angaben des Datums

Die englischen Wochentage und Monate werden immer großgeschriebeen. Beachte auch die Schreibweise der fettgedruckten Wörter.

Monday	Montag
Tuesday	Dienstag
Wednesday	Mittwoch
Thursday	Donnerstag
Friday	Freitag
Saturday	Samstag
Sunday	Sonntag

January	Januar
February	Februar
March	März
April	April
May	Mai
June	Juni
July	Juli
August	August
September	September
October	Oktober
November	November
December	Dezember

Im Englischen sprechen wir das Datum anders aus, als wir es schreiben. Daher merke dir den Unterschied:

Wir schreiben	Wir sagen
on 6 June *on 6th June*	*on the sixth of June*
on June 6th	*on June the sixth*
on Monday, 6th June	*on Monday, the sixth of June*

Nach dem Wochentag kommt immer ein Komma.

Wir sprechen Jahreszahlen in zwei Zehnereinheiten aus:

1752	*seventeen fifty-two*
1998	*nineteen ninety-eight*

Beachte: Eine Ausnahme bilden die ersten neun Jahre eines neuen Jahrhunderts:

2000	*two thousand*
2004	*two thousand and four*
2009	*two thousand and nine*

2010	*twenty ten*
2011	*twenty eleven*

Überprüfe hier, ob das Wissen sitzt

1 Bob liest die nächsten Fußballspieltermine vor.
Wie spricht er die Daten aus?

a June 12 — *the twelfth of June*

b April 1 — ______________________

c August 23 — ______________________

d January 31 — ______________________

e December 20 — ______________________

f November 3 — ______________________

2 Wie werden diese gesprochenen Daten geschrieben?

on the twenty-third of March — a *on 23rd March*

on the thirteenth of May — b ______________________

on the seventh of September — c ______________________

on the second of October — d ______________________

on the first of February — e ______________________

on the twenty-ninth of May — f ______________________

TESTEN • TESTEN • TESTEN • TESTEN • TESTEN • TESTEN • TESTEN

3 Amy liest Geburtstagstermine vor. Schreibe auf, was sie sagt. Schau auf die Liste.

Adam 9.1.	Tom 21.3.	Kirsty 16.5.
	Miss Jones 10.4.	
Colin 12.7.	Mrs Cobb 4.8.	Amy 8.9.

a Adam's birthday is on *the ninth of January.*

b Tom's is on ____________________

c Miss Jones' is ____________________

d Kirsty's ____________________

e Colin's ____________________

f Mrs Cobb's ____________________

g My birthday ____________________

And when is your birthday?

My birthday is ____________________

1
a (the twelfth of June)
b April the first/the first of April
c August the twenty-third/the twenty-third of August
d January the thirty-first/the thirty-first of January
e December the twentieth/the twentieth of December
f November the third/the third of November

2
a (on 23rd March)
b on 13th May
c on 7th September
d on 2nd October
e on 1st February
f on 29th May

3
a (the ninth of January)
b the twenty-first of March
c on the tenth of April
d is on the sixteenth of May
e is on the twelfth of July
f is on the fourth of August
g is ('s) on the eighth of September

29

Das *simple present* von *be* und die Verneinung

■ Das *simple present* von *be*

*Kate: **I am/I'm** 12 years old.*
Kate: Ich bin 12 Jahre alt.

*Kate's friend Mary **is** 12, too.*
Kates Freundin Mary ist auch zwölf.

*They **are**/They'**re** in the same class.*
Sie sind in derselben Klasse.

Langform	Kurzform	
I am	*I'm*	ich bin
you are	*you're*	du bist, Sie sind
he is	*he's*	er ist
she is	*she's*	sie ist
it is	*it's*	er/sie/es ist
we are	*we're*	wir sind
you are	*you're*	ihr seid, Sie sind
they are	*they're*	sie sind

In den Beispielen stehen Formen von *be* allein. Es ist also ein Vollverb.

Im modernen Englisch benutzen wir grundsätzlich die Kurzform in Unterhaltungen und privaten Briefen, E-Mails usw.

Die Verneinung des *simple present* von *be*

Um eine Form der Gegenwart von *be* zu verneinen, setzen wir *not/n't* unmittelbar dahinter, genau wie bei „sein" im Deutschen.
Tipp: Im modernen Englisch benutzen wir meist die Kurzform *isn't/aren't* mit Personalpronomen.
Die Langformen *is not/are not* klingen sehr formell.
*Kate: I **am not**/I'**m not** 13 yet.*
Kate: Ich bin noch nicht dreizehn.

*Mary **is not/isn't** Ann's best friend.*
Mary ist nicht Anns beste Freundin.

*The car **is not/isn't** in the garage.*
Das Auto ist nicht in der Garage.

*We **are not/aren't** hungry at the moment.*
Im Moment haben wir keinen Hunger.

*Kate and Mary **are not/aren't** in the basketball team.*
Kate und Mary sind nicht in der Basketballmannschaft.

Langform	Kurzform
I am not	*I'm not*
you are not	*you're not/aren't*
he is not	*he's not/isn't*
she is not	*she's not/isn't*
it is not	*it's not/isn't*
we are not	*we're not/aren't*
you are not	*you're not/aren't*
they are not	*they're not/aren't*

Überprüfe hier, ob das Wissen sitzt

1 Setze die richtige Form von *be* ein. Benutze aber bitte nur die Langform.

My name is Bob Parker. I _______ a pupil at Green Park School in Kingston. Kingston _______ a town near London. My friends _______ Tom and Amy Cobb. They _______ pupils at Green Park, too. I _______ captain of the Green Park football team, and Tom _______ the goal-keeper *(Torwart)*. He _______ quite good, but I _______ the star. And Amy? She _______ great. She _______ also my girlfriend and head *(Leiterin)* of my fan club.

2 Die Sätze sind alle sachlich falsch. Verneine sie mit der Lang- oder Kurzform und du bekommst richtige Aussagen.

a London is in Scotland.
No, that's wrong. London is not/isn't in Scotland.

b Hamburgers are very good for you.
Oh, no. They ________________ at all good for you.

c The Rhine is the longest river in Europe.
That's not right. The Rhine ________________ the longest river in Europe.

d Hamsters are dangerous animals.
That's silly. Hamsters ________________ dangerous.

e Tom is the captain of the football team.
No, that's wrong. Bob is the captain of the football team and Tom ________________ captain of the team.

f You are late again, Tom.
No, Sir. I ________________ late. It's only 10 o'clock.

3 Ergänze die Sätze durch eine Verneinung.

a Kirsty is Amy's girlfriend, but she _is not/isn't_ Adam's girlfriend.

b England is big, but it ________________ the biggest country in Europe.

c Hamsters are small animals, but elephants ________________ small animals.

d The Cobbs' dog ________________ called Coco. It's called Spooky.

e Cars are fast, but they ________________ faster than planes.

f Tom is good at sport, but he ________________ good at maths.

g Vegetables are good for you, but sweets ________________ good for you.

h The weather is warm in summer, but it ________________ warm in winter.

1 (My name is Bob Parker.) I am a pupil at Green Park School in Kingston. Kingston is a town near London. My friends are Tom and Amy Cobb. They are pupils at Green Park, too. I am captain of the Green Park football team, and Tom is the goalkeeper. He is quite good, but I am the star. And Amy? She is great. She is also my girlfriend and head of my fan club.

2 b Oh, no. They are not/aren't at all good for you.
c That's not right. The Rhine is not/isn't the longest river in Europe.
d That's silly. Hamsters are not/aren't dangerous.
e No, that's wrong. Bob is the captain of the football team and Tom is not/isn't captain of the team.
f No, Sir. I am not/I'm not late.

3 b England is big, but it is not/isn't the biggest country in Europe.
c Hamsters are small animals, but elephants are not/aren't small animals.
d The Cobbs' dog is not/isn't called Coco. It's called Spooky.
e Cars are fast, but they are not/aren't faster than planes.
f Tom is good at sport, but he is not/isn't good at maths.
g Vegetables are good for you, but sweets are not/aren't good for you.
h The weather is warm in summer, but it is not/isn't warm in winter.

Die Fragebildung und die Befehlsform von *be*

Die Fragebildung von *be*

Fragen bilden wir genau wie bei „sein" im Deutschen, indem wir das Subjekt mit der Verbform tauschen.

Are you *in the football team, Ben?*
Bist du in der Fußballmannschaft, Ben?

Is Ben *in Kate's class?*
Ist Ben in Kates Klasse?

Are Ben and Joshua *brothers?*
Sind Ben und Joshua Brüder?

Die Befehlsform von *be*

Bei Bitten und Befehlen stellen wir einfach *be* bzw. *don't be* an den Anfang des Satzes.

Please ***be*** *quiet, Ben. Kate's on the phone.*
Sei bitte ruhig, Ben. Kate telefoniert.

Don't ***be*** *late for your music lesson, Mary.*
Komme nicht zu spät zu deiner Musikstunde, Mary.

Überprüfe hier, ob das Wissen sitzt

1 Bilde Fragen.

a Amy is a good pupil.

Is Amy a good pupil?

b Bob is Amy's brother.

______________________________?

c Amy and Bob are good friends.

______________________________?

d I am in the team for the next match.

______________________________?

2 Der arme Adam Clarke macht anscheinend gar nichts richtig. Sage bitte Adam mit *be/don't be,* wie er sein und nicht sein soll.

a so noisy/quiet

Don't be so noisy, Adam. Be quiet, please.

b so lazy/helpful *(hilfsbereit)*

____________ so lazy, Adam. ____________, please.

c so naughty *(ungezogen)*/good

____________ so naughty, Adam. ____________, please.

d so silly/sensible *(vernünftig)*

____________, Adam. ____________, please.

1 b Is Bob Amy's brother?
c Are Amy and Bob good friends?
d Am I in the team for the next match?

2 b Don't be so lazy, Adam. Be helpful, please.
c Don't be so naughty, Adam. Be good, please.
d Don't be so silly, Adam. Be sensible, please.

Das *simple present* von *do* und die Verneinung

Ben: I always ***do*** *my homework at once.*
Ben: Ich mache meine Hausaufgaben immer sofort.

Mrs Green normally ***does*** *her shopping on Fridays.*
Normalerweise erledigt Frau Green ihre Einkäufe freitags.

Our neighbours ***do*** *a lot of gardening in the summer.*
Unsere Nachbarn machen im Sommer viel Gartenarbeit.

I	*do*	ich mache/erledige
you	*do*	du machst/erledigst
		Sie machen/erledigen
he	*does*	er macht/erledigt
she	*does*	sie macht/erledigt
it	*does*	er/sie/es macht/erledigt
we	*do*	wir machen/erledigen
you	*do*	ihr macht/erledigt
		Sie machen/erledigen
they	*do*	sie machen/erledigen

In den Beispielsätzen steht *do* allein. Es ist also ein Vollverb.

Als Vollverb bedeutet *do* „machen" oder „erledigen".
Tipp: Oft werden *make* und *do* verwechselt. Merke dir daher die folgenden Bedeutungen.

- „machen" im Sinne von: etwas erledigen
  Please ***do*** *your homework first.*
  Mach bitte zuerst deine Hausaufgaben.

- „machen" im Sinne von: etwas herstellen
  Frank ***makes*** *wonderful cakes.*
  Frank macht wunderbaren Kuchen.

Die Verneinung des *simple present* von *do*

Um das *simple present* von *do* als Vollverb zu verneinen, setzen wir *do not/ does not* bzw. *don't/doesn't* als Hilfsverb unmittelbar vor den Infinitiv. Wir benutzen grundsätzlich die Kurzform in der gesprochenen Sprache, also in Unterhaltungen, und in privaten Briefen, E-Mails usw.

*Kate: I **do not/don't** do the cooking during the week.*
Kate: Während der Woche koche ich nicht.

*Ben often **does not/doesn't** do his homework on time.*
Oft macht Ben seine Hausaufgaben nicht rechtzeitig.

*The boys **do not/don't do** the shopping at all.*
Die Jungen erledigen überhaupt keine Einkäufe.

Tipp: Wenn wir *do* als Vollverb benutzen, bilden wir die Verneinung und Fragen ebenfalls mit *do*. Daher kommt *do* natürlich zweimal im Satz vor, einmal als Hilfsverb und einmal als Vollverb.

Langform	Kurzform
I do not	*I don't*
you do not	*you don't*
he does not	*he doesn't*
she does not	*she doesn't*
it does not	*it doesn't*
we do not	*we don't*
you do not	*you don't*
they do not	*they don't*

■ Überprüfe hier, ob das Wissen sitzt

1 Setze die richtige Form von *do* in die Sätze ein.

a Bob often _______ sport on Saturdays.

b Harry Potter sometimes _______ magic tricks.

c When Mrs Cobb is ill, the children _______ the housework.

d At school, Kirsty _______ a test every month.

e Spooky and Coco _______ tricks sometimes.

f In Britain, small children _______ their homework at school.

2 Die Sätze unten sind sachlich falsch.
Stelle sie richtig mithilfe der Angaben in Klammern.

a Bob plays basketball. (football)

Bob *does not (doesn't)* play basketball. He *plays* football.

b Mr Cobb works in London. (Kingston)

Mr Cobb ________________ in London. He ________________ in Kingston.

c Mrs Nunn drives a train. (a bus)

Mrs Nunn ________________ a train. She ________________ a bus.

d Bob und Tom live in Ash Street. (Oak Lane)

Bob and Tom ________________ in Ash Street.

They ________________ in Oak Lane.

e Adam eats a lot of fruit. (sweets)

Adam ________________ much fruit. He _________ a lot of sweets.

TESTEN • TESTEN • TESTEN • TESTEN • TESTEN • TESTEN • TESTEN

3 Übersetze die folgenden Sätze ins Englische. Achte vor allem auf die unterstrichenen Teile.

a Tom und Bob spielen nicht Handball.

____

b Samstags gehen Kinder nicht zur Schule in Großbritannien.

____

c Amy und Tom wohnen nicht in der Green Road.

____

d Montags gehe ich nicht ins Kino.

____

e Kirsty spielt nicht Fußball.

____

f Sonntags macht ihr nicht eure Hausaufgaben.

____

1 a Bob often does sport on Saturdays.
b Harry Potter sometimes does magic tricks.
c When Mrs Cobb is ill, the children do the housework.
d At school, Kirsty does a test every month.
e Spooky and Coco do tricks sometimes.
f In Britain, small children do their homework at school.

2 b Mr Cobb does not/doesn't work in London. He works in Kingston.
c Mrs Nunn does not/doesn't drive a train. She drives a bus.
d Bob and Tom do not/don't live in Ash St. They live in Oak Lane.
e Adam does not/doesn't eat much fruit. He eats a lot of sweets.

3 a Tom and Bob do not/don't play handball.
b In Britain, children do not/don't go to school on Saturday.
c Amy and Tom do not/don't live in Green Road.
d I do not/don't go to the cinema on Monday.
e Kirsty does not/doesn't play football.
f You do not/don't do your homework on Sunday.

32

Die Fragebildung und die Befehlsform von *do*

Die Fragebildung von *do*

Fragen bilden wir mit *do/does* als Hilfsverb genau wie bei allen anderen Vollverben außer *be*. Genau wie bei der Verneinung kommt auch hier *do* zwei Mal vor, einmal als Hilfsverb, um die Frage zu bilden, und einmal als Vollverb.

Do *you* ***do*** *the shopping at the weekend, Ben?*
Erledigst du die Einkäufe am Wochenende, Ben?

Does *Mary* ***do*** *the cooking on Sundays?*
Kocht Mary sonntags?

Do *the Greens* ***do*** *a lot of gardening?*
Machen die Greens viel Gartenarbeit?

Die Befehlsform von *do*

Bei Bitten und Befehlen stellen wir einfach *do* bzw. *don't do* an den Anfang des Satzes.

Do *the shopping, please, Ben.*
Mach bitte die Einkäufe, Ben.

Don't do *your homework during lessons, Mary.*
Mach deine Hausaufgaben nicht während des Unterrichts, Mary.

Überprüfe hier, ob das Wissen sitzt

Bilde Fragen mit *do/does* und schreibe die passende Kurzantwort dazu.

a Jack thinks he is a great football player. (Bob?)

Does Bob think he is a great football player? Yes, *he does*.

b The boys live in Oak Lane. (girls?)

______________________ in Oak Lane?

Yes, they ______________________.

c Peter likes Old Carter. (Adam?)

______________________ like Old Carter.

No, he ______________________.

d English children do their homework after school. (German children?)

______________________ their homework after school?

Yes, ______________________.

e Jenny and Laura do sports every day. (Bob and Tom?)

______________________ sports every day?

No, ______________________.

b Do the girls live in Oak Lane?
Yes, they do.
c Does Adam like Old Carter?
No, he doesn't.
d Do German children do their homework after school? Yes, they do.
e Do Bob and Tom do sports every day? No, they don't.

33

Das *simple present* von *have (got)*

Das *simple present* von *have (got)* bilden wir wie folgt:

Langform	Kurzform	
I have (got)	*I've (got)*	ich habe
you have (got)	*you've (got)*	du hast, Sie haben
he has (got)	*he's (got)*	er hat
she has (got)	*she's (got)*	sie hat
it has (got)	*it's (got)*	es hat
we have (got)	*we've (got)*	wir haben
you have (got)	*you've (got)*	ihr habt, Sie haben
they have (got)	*they've (got)*	sie haben

Bedeutet *have* „haben" oder „besitzen", können wir *got* hinzufügen. Hat *have* eine andere deutsche Bedeutung, dann steht es allein.

Wir benutzen grundsätzlich die Kurzform in der gesprochenen Sprache, also in Unterhaltungen, in privaten Briefen, E-Mails usw.
*Tom: I **have (got)** a new bike.*
Tom: Ich habe ein neues Fahrrad.

*Mary: I always **have** breakfast before I go to school.*
Mary: Ich frühstücke immer, bevor ich in die Schule gehe.

*Kate **has (got)** a dog.*
Kate hat einen Hund.

*Ben just **has** a cup of coffee before he goes to school.*
Ben trinkt nur eine Tasse Kaffee, bevor er zur Schule geht.

*The Greens **have (got)** a big garden.*
Die Greens haben einen großen Garten.

Überprüfe hier, ob das Wissen sitzt

1 Setze die Langform der Gegenwart von *have* ein.

On Wednesdays, Amy has maths in the morning, then she ________ history. At eleven o'clock the whole school ________ a break *(Pause)*. Then her class ________ English. At lunchtime, Amy meets her friends and they all ________ lunch together. In the afternoon, she ________ sport and then her music lesson. "We ________ a very busy day on Wednesdays," she tells her mother.

2 Setze die Langform der Gegenwart von *have* ein. Benutze *have got,* wenn *have* eindeutig „besitzen" bedeutet.

The Cobbs have got a house. Amy and Tom ________________ a little dog called Spooky. Spooky always ________________ a lot of fun with the other dogs in Green Park. Sometimes they ________________ a race. And Amy always ________________ a good time with her friend Kirsty. When Spooky is dirty he ________________ a bath when they are at home again.

Amy and Tom ________________ a budgie, too. Its name is Tweets.

1 On Wednesdays, Amy (has) maths in the morning, then she has history. At eleven o'clock the whole school has a break. Then her class has English. At lunchtime, Amy meets her friends and they all have lunch together. In the afternoon, she has sport and then her music lesson. "We have a very busy day on Wednesdays", she tells her mother.

2 The Cobbs (have got) a house. Amy and Tom have got a little dog called Spooky. Spooky always has a lot of fun with the other dogs in Green Park. Sometimes they have a race. And Amy always has a good time with her friend Kirsty. When Spooky is dirty he has a bath when they are at home again.
Amy and Tom have got a budgie, too. Its name is Tweets.

34

Die Verneinung von *have got* und *have*

Die Verneinung von *have got*

Um *have got* zu verneinen, stellen wir *not/n't* unmittelbar hinter *have/has*. Das Wörtchen *got* bleibt dabei unverändert:

Langform	Kurzform
I have not got	*I haven't got*
you have not got	*you haven't got*
he has not got	*he hasn't got*
she has not got	*she hasn't got*
it has not got	*it hasn't got*
we have not got	*we haven't got*
you have not got	*you haven't got*
they have not got	*they haven't got*

Ben: I ***have not got/haven't got*** *a new bike.*
Ben: Ich habe kein neues Fahrrad.

Mary ***has not got/hasn't got*** *a dog.*
Mary hat keinen Hund.

They ***have not got/haven't got*** *a big garden.*
Sie haben keinen großen Garten.

■ Die Verneinung von *have*

Steht *have* allein – also ohne *got* –, dann bilden wir die Verneinung mit *do/does*, wie bei anderen Vollverben:

Langform	Kurzform
I do not have	*I don't have*
you do not have	*you don't have*
he does not have	*he doesn't have*
she does not have	*she doesn't have*
it does not have	*it doesn't have*
we do not have	*we don't have*
you do not have	*you don't have*
they do not have	*they don't have*

*Ben: I **do not have** breakfast before I go to school.*
Ben: Ich frühstücke nicht, bevor ich zur Schule gehe.

*Tom **does not have/doesn't have** coffee for breakfast.*
He has a glass of milk.
Tom trinkt keinen Kaffee zum Frühstück.
Er trinkt ein Glas Milch.

*The Greens **do not have/don't have** a big garden.*
Die Greens haben keinen großen Garten.

Wir benutzen grundsätzlich die Kurzform in der gesprochenen Sprache, also in Unterhaltungen, in privaten Briefen, E-Mails usw.

Beachte, dass die Kurzformen von *he/she/it is* und *he/she/it has* dieselben sind: *he's, she's it's*. Die Bedeutung der Kurzform ist jedoch leicht zu erkennen.

Überprüfe hier, ob das Wissen sitzt

1 Bilde verneinte Sätze mit der Lang- oder Kurzform wie vorgegeben.

a Amy has tea in the afternoon.

Amy does not/doesn't have tea in the afternoon.

b Mr and Mrs Cobb have a car.

Mr and Mrs Cobb ______________________________ a car.

c Mrs Nunn has a lot of time.

Mrs Nunn ______________________________ a lot of time.

d Kirsty has milk for breakfast.

Kirsty ______________________________ milk for breakfast.

e Bob and Tom have a good time at the youth club every week.

Bob and Tom __________ a good time at the youth club every week.

f We have a Chinese meal on Saturdays.

We ______________________ a Chinese meal on Saturdays.

g I have a shower every morning.

I ______________________________ a shower every morning.

2 Setze die verneinte Form von *have* ein.

At the weekend Tom doesn't have school, which means he __________ __________ maths and he __________ history. "I __________ school today!," says Tom, "I __________ anything to do! It's great." "You __________ school today, Tom, and you __________ any homework, but your grandparents need a few things from the shop. They __________ much food at home and they __________ time to do the shopping."

3 Bilde verneinte Sätze mit der Lang- oder Kurzform von *have got*.

a Amy has got a new coat.

Amy *has not got/hasn't got* a new coat.

b Tom Cobb has got a new bike.

Tom Cobb ______________________________ a new bike.

c Tom and Amy have got lots of video games.

Tom and Amy ______________________________ lots of video games.

d I have got a felt tip.

____

e Adam has got a new cap.

____

f The Parkers have got a swimming pool.

____

1 b Mr and Mrs Cobb do not/don't have a car.
c Mrs Nunn does not/doesn't have a lot of time.
d Kirsty does not/doesn't have milk for breakfast.
e Bob and Tom do not/don't have a good time at the youth club every week.
f We do not/don't have a Chinese meal on Saturdays.
g I do not/don't have a shower every morning.

2 At the weekend Tom doesn't have school, which means he doesn't have maths and he doesn't have history. "I don't have school today!," says Tom, "I don't have anything to do! It's great."
"You don't have school today, Tom, and you don't have any homework, but your grandparents need a few things from the shop. They don't have much food at home and they don't have time to do the shopping."
(Für *doesn't have* kannst du auch *does not have* einsetzen; für *don't have* auch *do not have*.)

3 b Tom Cobb has not/hasn't got a new bike.
c Tom and Amy have not/haven't got lots of video games.
d I have not/haven't got a felt tip.
e Adam has not/hasn't got a new cap.
f The Parkers have not/haven't got a swimming pool.

35

Die Fragestellung bei *have got* und *have*

Die Fragestellung bei *have got*

Bei *have got* bilden wir Fragen durch den Austausch von Subjekt und *have/has*, genau wie bei „haben" im Deutschen.

***Have** you **got** a dog, Kate?*
Hast du einen Hund, Kate?

***Has** Mary **got** a sister?*
Hat Mary eine Schwester?

***Have** the Greens **got** any children?*
Haben die Green Kinder?

Die Fragestellung bei *have*

Steht *have* allein – also ohne *got* –, bilden wir Fragen mit *do/does* genau wie bei allen anderen Vollverben.

***Do** you **have** a dog, Kate?*
Hast du einen Hund, Kate?

***Does** Mary **have** a sister?*
Hat Mary eine Schwester?

***Do** the Greens **have** any children?*
Haben die Greens Kinder?

Überprüfe hier, ob das Wissen sitzt

1 Bilde Fragen wie in den folgenden Beispielsätzen vorgegeben.

a Amy has milk with her tea.

Does Amy have milk with her tea?

b Mr and Mrs Cobb have lunch together every day.

Do Mr and Mrs Cobb have lunch together every day?

c Tom Cobb has football practice every week.

______________________ football practice every week?

d Tom and Bob have a shower after football practice.

______________________ a shower after football practice?

2 Bilde Fragesätze wie im Beispiel vorgegeben.

a Tom and Amy have got a budgie.

Have Tom and Amy got a budgie?

Yes, they have.

b Kirsty has got a CD player.

____

Yes, she has.

c Mr and Mrs Clarke have got a car.

____

Yes, they have.

1 c Does Tom Cobb have football practice every week?
d Do Tom and Bob have a shower after football practice?
2 b Has Kirsty got a CD player?
c Have Mr and Mrs Clarke got a car?

36

Modale Hilfsverben – allgemeine Merkmale

Wir benutzen modale Hilfsverben wie *can* und *must* mit einem Vollverb ohne *to:*
*You **can watch** TV now.*
Du kannst jetzt fernsehen.

*Ben **must come** home at once.*
Ben muss sofort nach Hause kommen.

Anders als im Deutschen ist es im Englischen nicht möglich, ein modales Hilfsverb ohne Vollverb zu benutzen:
*Gemma **can speak** Spanish.*
Gemma kann Spanisch (sprechen).

*Mary **must go** to the doctor's today.*
Mary muss heute zum Arzt (gehen).

Modale Hilfsverben haben bei allen Personen die gleiche Form. Anders als bei Vollverben und bei den Hilfsverben *be, have* und *do* hat die 3. Person Singular *(he/she/it)* keine -*s*-Endung:
*Ben **can play** football very well.*
Ben kann sehr gut Fußball spielen.

*Kate **needn't do** her homework now.*
Kate muss jetzt ihre Hausaufgaben nicht machen.

Wie bei den Hilfsverben *be, have and do* bilden wir die Verneinung und Fragen ohne *do/does/did:*
*Kate **must not spend** so much money.*
Kate darf nicht so viel Geld ausgeben.

Can** Ben **dance?
Kann Ben tanzen?

Wir können die modalen Hilfsverben nur im Präsens und mit zukünftiger Bedeutung benutzen:

- Präsens
  *We **can eat now.***
  Wir können jetzt essen.

- Zukunft
  *We **can eat** out **tomorrow.***
  Morgen können wir essen gehen.

- Präsens
  *I **must phone** Mary **now.***
  Ich muss jetzt Mary anrufen.

- Zukunft
  *I **must wash** the car **tomorrow.***
  Morgen muss ich das Auto waschen.

Nur *can* hat eine eigene Form der Vergangenheit *(past)*, nämlich *could*. Wollen wir die anderen modalen Hilfsverben in der Vergangenheit benutzen, müssen wir ein geeignetes Ersatzverb gebrauchen:
*Ben **could** not go to school yesterday.*
Ben konnte gestern nicht zur Schule gehen.

*He **had to stay** at home because he was ill.*
Er musste zu Hause bleiben, weil er krank war.

Überprüfe hier, ob das Wissen sitzt

1 Sieh dir die Tabelle an, um zu sagen, was Mr and Mrs Cobb können bzw. nicht können. Benutze nur *can/can't*.

	speak German	drive a car	bake a cake	swim	repair a chair
Mr Cobb	✘	✔	✘	✘	✔
Mrs Cobb	✘	✔	✔	✔	✘

a Mr Cobb *can't speak* German, he ______ a cake and he ______, but he ______ a car and he ______ a chair.

b Mrs Cobb ______ German and she ______ a chair, but she ______ a car, she ______ a cake and she ______.

2 Setze *must* oder *needn't* in die Sätze ein.

a We ____________ take an umbrella. It has stopped raining.

b You ____________ wash your hands before you eat.

c We ____________ answer all of the questions, only three of them.

d We ____________ be at the airport by 5 o'clock or we will miss *(verpassen)* the flight.

3 Beantworte die folgenden Fragen mit *yes*. Dann frage noch mal und antworte mit *no*, aber diesmal in der Vergangenheitsform. Verwende dabei die richtige Form von *not be able to* für die Antworten.

a Can Miss Jones drive a car?

Yes, *she can*.

Could she drive a car ten years ago? No, she *couldn't*.

b Can Adam swim?

Yes, he ______.

______ when he was a baby?

No, he ______.

c Can Tom skateboard?

Yes, ______.

______ last year?

No, he ______.

d Can you ride a bike?

Yes, I ______.

______ you ______ when you started school?

______, I ______.

1 a Mr Cobb (can't speak) German, he can't bake a cake and he can't swim, but he can drive a car and he can repair a chair.
b Mrs Cobb can't speak German and she can't repair a chair, but she can drive a car, she can bake a cake and she can swim.
2 a We needn't take an umbrella. It has stopped raining.
b You must wash your hands before you eat.
c We needn't answer all of the questions, only three of them.
d We must be at the airport by 5 o'clock or we will miss the flight.
3 b Yes, he can.
Could he swim when he was a baby?
No, he couldn't.
c Yes, he can.
Could he skateboard last year?
No, he couldn't.
e Yes, I can.
Could you ride a bike when you started school?
Yes, I could. (No, I couldn't.)

TESTEN • TESTEN • TESTEN • TESTEN • TESTEN • TESTEN • TESTEN • TESTEN • TESTEN • TESTEN

37

Modale Hilfsverben im Einzelnen

■ ***Must/have to*** **(müssen)**

Im normalen Gebrauch benutzen wir das Ersatzverb *have to* für „müssen“:

*I **have to visit** my grandparents on Sundays.*

Ich muss meine Großeltern sonntags besuchen.

Wollen wir eine wichtige Verpflichtung ausdrücken, gebrauchen wir *must:*

*We **must go to** school every day.*

Wir müssen jeden Tag zur Schule gehen.

Beachte: Da *must* keine eigene Vergangenheit hat, benutzen wir *had to/ did not have to* als Ersatzverb:

*We **had to walk** to school yesterday.*

Gestern mussten wir zur Schule laufen.

*I **didn't have to** help my dad.*

Ich musste meinem Papa nicht helfen.

Must not/need not/do not have to (nicht dürfen/nicht müssen)

Wir benutzen *must not/mustn't,* um ein Verbot auszudrücken:

*They **mustn't drive** so fast here.*

Hier dürfen sie nicht so schnell fahren.

Wollen wir sagen, dass es keine Verpflichtung oder Notwendigkeit gibt, benutzen wir *need not/needn't* oder das Ersatzverb *do not/don't have to:*

*I **needn't/don't have to** do my homework today.*

Ich muss heute meine Hausaufgaben nicht machen.

■ *Can/be able to* (können)

Wir benutzen *can* oder das Ersatzverb *be able to*, um eine Fähigkeit auszudrücken:

*Sam **can understand** some German, but he isn't able to speak it.*
Sam kann etwas Deutsch verstehen, aber er kann es nicht sprechen.

Wir benutzen *can* oder das Ersatzverb *be allowed to*, um eine Erlaubnis auszudrücken:

*We **can/are allowed** to go home now.*
Wir können jetzt nach Hause gehen.

Die Vergangenheit von *can* ist *could*:

*We **could go home** early yesterday.*
Gestern konnten wir früh nach Hause gehen.

Bedeutung	Modale Hilfsverben		Ersatzverb
	Englisch	Deutsch	
Fähigkeit	*can/could*	können/konnten	*be able to*
Erlaubnis	*can/could*	können/konnten	*be allowed to*
Verbot	*must not*	nicht dürfen	*not be allowed to*
Verpflichtung	*must*	müssen	*have to*
freie Wahl	*needn't*	nicht müssen nicht brauchen	*not have to*

Überprüfe hier, ob das Wissen sitzt

1 Sieh dir die Klammern an und setze *can, must, needn't, mustn't* oder *may* ein.

a You mustn't eat ice cream in the shop. *(kein Eis im Laden!)*

b We __________ feed *(füttern)* the monkeys at 4 o'clock, but we __________ feed them at 2 o'clock. *(Fütterung nicht um 4, sondern um 2 Uhr)*

c On Wednesday the children __________ go home at 3 o'clock, but on Mondays they __________ stay until 4.30. *(montags bis 4.30, sonst bis 3 Uhr)*

d __________ we feed the dog, please? *(Hund füttern)*

e People __________ swim here, but you __________ have a picnic *if* you want. *(Schwimmen verboten, Picknicken erlaubt)*

f We __________ be quiet after 10 p.m., but we __________ go to bed. *(Zimmerlautstärke ab 10 p.m., aber noch keine Bettruhe)*

g Children __________ go into the bar, but they __________ wait in the children's room. *(Zutritt für Kinder in der Bar verboten)*

h __________ I go to the disco? *(Discobesuch)*

2 Setze *can, mustn't,* die richtige Form von *be allowed to* oder *Can ...?/ Could ...?/May ...?* in die Sätze ein. Achte dabei auf die Zeitform.

a You ______________________________ stay here, but you must be quiet.

b You ____ shout in the classroom.

c Adam _________________________________ go out yesterday. He was ill.

d _____________________________ I use your pen, please? – Yes, of course.

e Adam ______________________ eat so many sweets. He's much foo fat.

f ______ Bob ____________________ go to the concert next week?

Only if he is not ill.

g Kirsty and Adam ____________________ go to the disco yesterday because they had too much homework to do.

h We ______________________________ be late for school.

3 Lies dir zunächst die Dialoge und Sätze sorgfältig durch und kreuze dann die richtige Lösung an. Es gibt jeweils nur eine mögliche Antwort.

can/could, be able to, be allowed to

a – Julia is allowed to speak ☐ can speak ☐ German.
– You're right. She'll be allowed to help ☐ 'll be able to help ☐ us when the German visitors are here.

b My father says I can't go ☐ can go ☐ on the trip unless I do better at school. If I don't, he won't give the permission and I won't be allowed to go ☐ am not able to go ☐.

c I was lucky yesterday. Mum phoned the hospital and they said I could come ☐ can come ☐ at once. They can see ☐ were able to see ☐ me because another patient couldn't come ☐ can't come ☐.

1 b mustn't – can   c can – must
d May/Can   e mustn't – can
f must – needn't   g mustn't – can
h May/Can

2 a You can/are allowed to stay here, but you must be quiet.
b You mustn't/aren't allowed to shout in the classroom.
c Adam wasn't allowed to go out yesterday. He was ill.
d Can/Could/May I use your pen, please? – Yes, of course.
e Adam mustn't eat so many sweets. He's much too fat.
f Will Bob be allowed to go to the concert next week? ...
g Kirsty and Adam were not allowed to go to the disco yesterday ...
h We mustn't be late for school.

3 a can – be able to
b can't – be allowed to
c could – were able to – couldn't

38

Simple present und *present progressive*

Simple present

Mit Ausnahme der 3. Person Singular hat das *simple present* immer dieselbe Form wie der Infinitiv. Bei *he/she/it* wird ein -*s* angehängt.
Beachte: Die Schreibregeln beim Anhängen von -*s* sind genau wie die für den regelmäßigen Plural.
Ist kein Hilfsverb im Satz, bilden wir die Verneinung mit *do not/don't* bzw. *does not/doesn't*. Das Vollverb steht bei der Verneinung immer im Infinitiv.
Gibt es kein Hilfsverb im Satz, bilden wir Fragen ebenfalls mit *do not/don't* bzw. *does not/doesn't*.
Wir benutzen das *simple present*, um zu sagen, was immer so ist oder was man immer wieder macht.

*The Kings **live** in London.*
Die Kings wohnen in London.

*Kate **practises** the guitar every day.*
Kate übt jeden Tag Gitarre.

*The Kings normally **have** a hot meal in the evening.*
Normalerweise essen die Kings abends eine warme Mahlzeit.

*Ben and Kate **do not/don't go** to school by bus.*
Ben und Kate fahren nicht mit dem Bus zur Schule.

*Mary, **do you live** in Albert Street, too?*
Mary, wohnst du auch in der Albert Street?

Mit dem *simple present* kommen die folgenden Zeitangaben sehr häufig vor: *always, never; often, seldom* (selten), *sometimes; usually, normally, generally* (im Allgemeinen); *every day/week/month/Christmas/...; on Mondays/ Tuesdays/...; at weekends/Easter/...*

Present progressive

Wir bilden das *present progressive* mit *am/is/are* + der -*ing*-Form des Vollverbs.Beachte folgende Schreibregeln bei der -*ing*-Form:

Bei Verben, die auf *-e* enden, entfällt das *-e:*

come	*coming*	*make*	*making*

Bei Verben, die auf *-ie* enden, wird das *-ie* zum *-y:*

lie	*lying*	liegen

Bei Verben, die mit einem kurzen Vokal + Konsonanten enden, verdoppeln wir den Konsonanten:

put	*putting*	*run*	*running*

Da es beim *present progressive* immer ein Hilfsverb, also *am/is/are,* gibt, bilden wir die Verneinung mit *not/'nt.*
Um Fragen zu bilden, tauschen wir *am/is/are* und das Subjekt einfach aus.
*Kate **is practising** the guitar at the moment.*
Kate übt im Moment Gitarre.

*The Kings **are doing** the shopping at present.*
Zurzeit kaufen die Kings ein.

*Mrs King **is not/isn't cooking.** She's in the garden.*
Mrs King kocht gerade nicht. Sie ist im Garten.

***Is** Ben **playing** football now?*
Spielt Ben gerade Fußball?

Die folgenden Verben haben normalerweise keine *progressive*-Form: *believe, hate, hear, know, like, love, mean, see, want.*

Wir benutzen das *present progressive* um zu sagen, was im Moment des Sprechens oder Schreibens tatsächlich passiert, und wenn wir Bilder beschreiben. Mit dem *present progressive* kommen folgende drei Zeitangaben vor:

at present	zurzeit
at the moment	im Moment
now	jetzt

Überprüfe hier, ob das Wissen sitzt

1 Setze die richtige Form des *simple present* in die Sätze ein.

a Ben always ________________ (go) to school by bus.

b ________________ (Kate/walk) to school?

c Mary ________________ (not like) sport very much.

d ________________ (British children/learn) French or German?

e We ________________ (not have) any lessons on Wednesday afternoons.

f The Snows ________________ (live) in Victoria Street.

g ________________ (you/enjoy) TV programmes about animals?

h Tom ________________ (spend) a lot of time playing computer games.

2 Setze die richtige Form des *present progressive* in die Sätze ein.

a ________________ (Kate and Mary/have) a music lesson at the moment?

b Kate's not her. She ________________ (take) the dog for a walk.

c ________________ (Ben/play) football now?

d Whenever I see Tom, he ________________ (sit) in front of the TV.

e Mum ________________ (not cook) at the moment.
She ________________ (cut) the grass.

f I ________________ (do) the washing-up and Kate ________________ (put) things away for me.

3 Setze die richtige Form der Gegenwart der angegebenen Verben in die Sätze ein.

Kirsty and Amy ________________ (do) their homework. But they ________________ (not/work) very hard. Kirsty ________________ (think) maths is boring and Amy ________________ (hate) history. Instead (stattdessen), they ________________ (choose) a film they want to see later. Amy and Kirsty both ________________ (like) cartoons.

1
- a Ben always goes to school by bus.
- b Does Kate walk to school?
- c Mary does not like sport very much.
- d Do British children learn French or German?
- e We do not have any lessons on Wednesday afternoons.
- f The Snows live in Victoria Street.
- g Do you enjoy TV programmes about animals?
- h Tom spends a lot of time playing computer games.

2
- a Are Kate and Mary having a music lesson at the moment?
- b She is taking the dog for a walk.
- c Is Ben playing football now?
- d Whenever I see Tom, he is sitting in front of the TV.
- e Mum is not cooking at the moment. She is cutting the grass.
- f I am doing the washing-up and Kate is putting things away for me.

3 Kirsty and Amy are doing their homework. But they are not working very hard. Kirsty thinks maths is boring and Amy hates history. Instead, they are choosing a film they want to see later. Amy and Kirsty both like cartoons.

39

Simple past

Beim *simple past* musst du zwischen regelmäßigen und unregelmäßigen Verben unterscheiden.
Bei regelmäßigen Verben hängen wir allen Personen ein *-ed* an den Infinitiv. Beachte diese Schreibregeln beim Anhängen von *-ed:*
Ein stummes, also nicht gesprochenes, *-e* entfällt:

bake	*baked*	*move*	*moved*
live	*lived*	*phone*	*phoned*

Das *-y* nach einem Konsonanten wird zum *-i:*

carry	*carried*
hurry	*hurried*
try	*tried*

Endet das Verb auf *-y* nach einem Vokal, bleibt das *-y* erhalten:

enjoy	*enjoyed*
play	*played*

Gibt es kein Hilfsverb im Satz, bilden wir die Verneinung mit *did not/didn't*.
Gibt es kein Hilfsverb im Satz, bilden wir Fragen ebenfalls mit did.
Wir benutzen das *simple past* für völlig abgeschlossene Handlungen in der Vergangenheit.

Ben ***played*** *football yesterday.*
Ben spielte gestern Fußball.

The Kings ***went*** *to the cinema last night.*
Gestern Abend gingen die Kings ins Kino.

Kate ***did not/didn't like*** *the film much.*
Kate mochte den Film nicht besonders.

Did *you* ***hear*** *that stupid man?*
Hast du den doofen Mann gehört?

WISSEN • WISSEN • WISSEN • WISSEN • WISSEN • WISSEN • WISSEN

Überprüfe hier, ob das Wissen sitzt

1 Setze die Verben in Klammern in der richtigen Form des *past tense* in die Sätze ein.

a The children built (build) a big sandcastle on the beach last summer.

b It ________ (rain) yesterday, so we ________ (stay) at home and ________ (play) indoor games.

c Last night we ________ (see) a good programme on TV.

d Yesterday Tom's uncle from America ________ (come) for two weeks.

e Last summer the Clarkes ________ (buy) a new car.

f I ________ (*Verneinung;* see) the accident.

2 Stelle Fragen. Wonach du fragen sollst, steht in den unterstrichenen Satzteilen.

a Miss Jones lived in Bonn in 1980.

When did Miss Jones live in Bonn?

b Last summer Tom went to Spain.

________ last summer?

c Yesterday I played volleyball.

________ you ________ yesterday?

1 b It rained yesterday, so we stayed at home and played indoor games.
c Last night we saw a good programme on TV.
d Yesterday Tom's uncle from America came for two weeks.
e Last summer the Clarkes bought a new car.
f I didn't see the accident.

2 b Where did Tom go last summer?
c What did you play yesterday?

40

Past progressive

Das *past progressive* bilden wir mit *was/were* und der *-ing*-Form des Vollverbs.
Da es bei dem *past progressive* immer ein Hilfsverb, also *was/were*, gibt, bilden wir die Verneinung mit *not/n't*.
Um Fragen zu bilden, tauschen wir *was/were* und das Subjekt einfach aus.
Wollen wir sagen, dass eine Handlung schon im Gange war, als ein neues Ereignis (plötzlich) eintrat, benutzen wir das *past progressive*.
Möchten wir sagen, dass eine Handlung zu einem bestimmten Zeitpunkt oder während eines bestimmten Zeitraumes im Gange war, gebrauchen wir ebenfalls das *past progressive*.
*I saw an accident when **I was walking** to school.*
Als ich zur Schule ging, sah ich einen Unfall.

*We **were playing** football at 3 o'clock last Saturday.*
Am letzten Samstag um 3 Uhr spielten wir gerade Fußball.

*Ben **was not/wasn't doing** his homework when I spoke to him.*
Als ich mit ihm sprach war Ben nicht dabei, seine Hausaufgabe zu machen.

***Were** the men **cleaning** the windows?*
Waren die Männer dabei, die Fenster zu putzen?

Folgende Verben haben normalerweise keine *progressive*-Form:

believe	glauben
hear	hören
like	mögen
mean	bedeuten
want	möchten

hate	hassen
know	wissen, kennen
love	lieben
see	sehen

Überprüfe hier, ob das Wissen sitzt

Suche Formen des *simple past* und des *past progressive* aus der Geschichte heraus. Mache dann zwei Listen mit der Infinitivform dieser Verben, regelmäßig und unregelmäßig. Schreibe auf einen Zettel.

There was nearly a bad accident in Albert Road on Saturday afternoon. Kate Snow, 13, was taking her dog, Luna, for a walk. She wanted to go to the park.

Kate was walking along the pavement when Luna suddenly saw a cat on the other side of the road. The cat, Oscar, was washing himself on a wall.

Luna pulled so hard that Kate let go. Luna was running across the road when a taxi came along. The taxi-driver, Jack Kemp, did not want to hit Luna, so he drove his taxi up on to the pavement. But he didn't see Mrs Betty Edwards with her baby, one-year-old Sharon, in a push-chair *(Kinderwagen)*.

The taxi hit the push-chair and knocked it over. Sharon fell out of the push-chair, but luckily nothing happened to her. She just laughed.

And Luna? She caught Oscar, but she soon felt sorry. They fought for a few minutes and Oscar won. He cut Luna's nose quite badly. Poor Luna. She chose the wrong cat. Let's hope it taught her a lesson.

unregelmäßige Verben:
be, take, see, let, run, come, drive, hit, fall, catch, feel, fight, win, cut, choose, teach

regelmäßige Verben:
want, walk, wash, pull, knock, happen, laugh

41

Present perfect

Das *present perfect* bilden wir mit *have/has* und der 3. Form (Partizip Perfekt) des Vollverbs.
Bei regelmäßigen Verben hat die 3. Form dieselbe Form wie die des *simple past,* also *infinitive* + *-ed.*
Wie beim *simple past* gibt es auch hier bestimmte Schreibregeln, die du beim Anhängen von *-ed* beachten musst:

- ein stummes *-e* fällt weg:
  *phon**e*** *phon**ed***
- das *-y* nach einem Konsonanten wird zum *-i* verwandelt:
  *empt**y*** *empt**ied***
- *-b, -d, -m, -p, -s* und *-t* werden nach einem einfachen Vokal verdoppelt:
  *dro**p*** *dro**pped***

Bei den unregelmäßigen Verben hat das Partizip eine eigene Form, die du auswendig lernen musst:
be ***been***

Wir bilden die Verneinung, indem wir *not/n't* unmittelbar nach *have/has* stellen.
Um Fragen zu bilden, tauschen wir *have/has* und das Subjekt einfach aus.

Wollen wir sagen, dass etwas passiert ist, ohne einen Zeitpunkt in der Vergangenheit zu nennen, benutzen wir das *present perfect.*
Oft benutzen wir das *present perfect* für Handlungen und Situationen, die irgendwann in der Vergangenheit begonnen haben, aber noch andauern. Diese Handlungen bzw. Situationen sind also noch nicht abgeschlossen.
*Kate **has bought** a new guitar.*
Kate hat eine neue Gitarre gekauft.

*The Kings **have lived** in London for ten years.*
Die Kings wohnen seit zehn Jahren in London.

*The bus still **has not/hasn't come.***
Der Bus ist immer noch nicht gekommen.

***Have** you **seen** the latest Harry Potter film yet?*
Hast du schon den neuesten Harry-Potter-Film gesehen?

Der genaue Zeitpunkt des Geschehens in der Vergangenheit wird nicht genannt. Nur der Bezug zur Gegenwart ist von Interesse.

Folgende Zeitadverbien treten häufig mit dem *present perfect* zusammen auf. Sie gelten also als Signalwörter für das *present perfect:*

already	– schon	*not ... yet*	– bis jetzt noch nicht
just	– gerade	*so far*	– bisher
ever	– jemals	*yet*	– bisher
never	– bisher noch nie		

Present perfect* oder *simple past?

Du musst das *simple past* verwenden, wenn es darauf ankommt, wann jemand etwas in der Vergangenheit getan hat oder wann etwas in der Vergangenheit geschah *(yesterday, in 1970, last week, ...).*
Du musst das *present perfect* verwenden, wenn das Ereignis einer Handlung oder ein Zustand bis in die Gegenwart hineinreicht, wenn also ein Bezug zur Gegenwart da ist.
*Tom **has broken** his leg. He **broke** it yesterday.*
Tom hat sich sein Bein gebrochen. Er brach es sich gestern.

*I **have bought** a great CD. I **bought** it last Saturday.*
Ich habe eine großartige CD gekauft. Ich kaufte sie letzten Samstag.

Überprüfe hier, ob das Wissen sitzt

1 Verwende die unten angegebenen Satzelemente, um Sätze mit dem *present perfect* zu bilden.

a Tom has just gone (just/go) home.

b We ______________________ (already/do) this exercise.

c Tom and Amy ______________ (not/finish) cleaning their rooms.

d I ______________________________ (never/see) a lion.

e Mr Carter ______________________ (never/be) to Wales.

f I ____________________________ (just/buy) a new pen.

g Amy and Kirsty ______________ (never/see) the Film „Grinch".

h Adam Clarke __________ (already/eat) two bags of sweets today.

2 Schreibe ganze verneinte Sätze im *present perfect*.

a Harry Potter/never like/his aunt and uncle

Harry Potter has never liked his aunt and uncle.

b The Parkers/never eat/a Spanish meal

____

c Mrs Clarke/not be/ill for many years

____

d Adam/not buy/any more sweets

____

e The Clarkes/not drive/their car for a long time

____

f Kirsty/not learn/the new dance yet

____

3 Setze die Verben in Klammern ins *present perfect* oder *simple past*.

Yesterday Tom ________________ (go) to school by bike. He ________________ (meet) Bob at school. „There's a new film at the cinema, 'The Grinche'. Do you want to go at the weekend?" he ________________ (ask) Bob. „No, I ___ (see) it already. I ________________ (see) it last month when I ________________ (be) on holiday in Manchester." „I ________________ (not see) it yet", ________________ (say) Amy. „The last film I ________________ (see) ________________ (be) 'Star Wars'." „Well, we ________________ (win) four free tickets to the cinema and mum ________________ (give) them to me."

1 b We have already done this exercise.
c Tom and Amy have not finished cleaning their rooms.
d I have never seen a lion.
e Mr Carter has never been to Wales.
f I have just bought a new pen.
g Amy and Kirsty have never seen the film „Grinch".
h Adam Clarke has already eaten two bags of sweets today.

2 b The Parkers have never eaten a Spanish meal.
c Mrs Clarke has not (hasn't) been ill for many years.
d Adam has not (hasn't) bought any more sweets.
e The Clarkes have not (haven't) driven their car for a long time.
f Kirsty has not (hasn't) learnt the new dance yet.

3 Yesterday Tom went to school by bike. He met Bob at school. „There's a new film at the cinema, 'The Grinch'. Do you want to go at the weekend?" he asked Bob. „No, I have seen it already. I saw it last month when I was on holiday in Manchester." „I have not seen it yet", said Amy. „The last film I saw was 'Star Wars'." „Well, we won four free tickets to the cinema and mum gave/has given them to me."

Present perfect mit *for/since*

Oft verwenden wir das *present perfect* für Handlungen und Situationen, die in der Vergangenheit angefangen haben, aber noch andauern. Sie sind also noch nicht völlig abgeschlossen. Im Deutschen verwenden wir in solchen Fällen das Präsens.

*Greg Hooper **has lived** here for over 60 years.*
Greg Hooper wohnt hier seit über 60 Jahren.

*We **have not had** a rainy day since Christmas.*
Seit Weihnachten haben wir keinen Regentag gehabt.

Bei der noch nicht abgeschlossenen Vergangenheit kommen folgende Zeitadverbien häufig vor:

*I have never seen this movie **before.***
Ich habe diesen Film bisher nicht gesehen.

*We have lived here **for** three years.*
Wir wohnen hier seit drei Jahren.

*We have lived here **since** last May.*
Wir wohnen hier seit letztem Mai.

*Have you **already** met Mary?*
Hast du Mary schon kennen gelernt?

*I have not finished **yet.***
Ich bin noch nicht fertig.

*Have you **ever** been to the USA?*
Warst du schon (einmal) in den USA?

*They have **never** been on holiday.*
Sie sind noch nie im Urlaub gewesen.

*Hank has **still** not got up.*
Hank ist immer noch nicht aufgestanden.

*We have had a lot of fun **till now.***
Bis jetzt haben wir viel Spaß gehabt.

Überprüfe hier, ob das Wissen sitzt

1 Handelt es sich bei den folgenden Zeitangaben um Zeiträume oder Zeitpunkte? Schreibe je nachdem *for* bzw. *since* dazu.

a ___________ ten o'clock
b ___________ Christmas
c ___________ last summer
d ___________ ten minutes
e ___________ one month
f ___________ the last lesson
g ___________ a long time
h ___________ a week

2 Setze *for* bzw. *since* und die richtige Form des *present perfect* in die Sätze ein.

a Joe has been (be) at this school for five years.
b Where's Alison? I ____________________ (not see) her ____________________ this morning.
c Mr Pryce ____________________ (know) his wife ____________________ they were both small children.
d Ben ____________________ (not see) his uncle ____________________ several years.
e I ____________________ (not be) very well ____________________ Monday.

1
a since ten o'clock
b since Christmas
c since last summer
d for ten minutes
e for one month
f since the last lesson
g for a long time
h for a week

2
b Where's Alison? I have not seen her since this morning.
c Mr Pryce has known his wife since they were both small children.
d Ben has not seen his uncle for several years.
e I haven't been very well since Monday.

43

Present perfect progressive

Form

Das *present perfect progressive* bilden wir mit *have/has* + *been* + der *-ing*-Form des Vollverbs.
Wir bilden die Verneinung durch das Einfügen von *not/n't* unmittelbar nach *have/has.*
Wollen wir Fragen bilden, tauschen wir *have/has* und das Subjekt einfach aus.

*I **have been waiting** for you since 5 o'clock.*
Ich warte seit 5 Uhr auf dich.

*Joe **has been playing** computer games for nearly three hours.*
Joe spielt seit fast drei Stunden Computerspiele.

*They **have not been** working all the time.*
Sie haben nicht die ganze Zeit gearbeitet.

***Have** you **been waiting** long?*
Warten Sie schon lange?

Gebrauch

Wir verwenden das *present perfect progressive* für länger andauernde Handlungen und Situationen, die zum Zeitpunkt des Sprechens noch andauern.
Im Deutschen benutzen wir in solchen Fällen meist das Präsens mit „schon", um zu verdeutlichen, dass die Handlung bzw. Situation bereits länger andauert:

*Dad **has been sleeping** for nearly ten hours.*
Papa schläft schon seit fast zehn Stunden.

*Clare and Joe **have been dancing** the whole time.*
Clare und Joe tanzen schon die ganze Zeit.

Ausnahmen

Beachte: Die folgenden Verben haben meist keine *progressive* Form, da sie keine Tätigkeiten, sondern Zustände und Gefühle ausdrücken:

believe	glauben
dislike	nicht mögen
hate	hassen
know	wissen, kennen
like	mögen
love	lieben, sehr mögen
mean	meinen
notice	bemerken
see	(mit dem Auge) sehen
seem	scheinen
want	wollen
wish	wünschen

Überprüfe hier, ob das Wissen sitzt

1 Bilde Fragen und verneinte Antworten, wie im Beispiel vorgegeben.

a Bob/read/for a long time

Has Bob been reading for a long time?

No, Bob has not been reading for a long time.

b they/work/here very long

____

____

c Alan/climb/mountains since 2000

____

____

d Jim/take/photos all afternoon

____

____

e Sue/play/the guitar for two years

____

____

f Colin/play/football since breakfast

____

____

2 Setze die Verben in Klammern in die Sätze ein. Benutze durchweg das *present perfect progressive*.

a Sally has been doing (do) the test for 45 minutes.

b The sun ____________________ (shine) since early morning.

c We ____________________ (lie) in the garden for three hours.

d Freddy ____________________ (learn) irregular verbs for ten minutes.

e It ____________________ (rain) for four days now. What a holiday!

f Alison and Jack ____________________ (play) tennis for two hours.

g George ____________________ (download) files from the Internet since 5 o'clock.

h Mrs Pryce ____________________ (try) to phone her friend in the USA for 30 minutes, bus she can't get through.

1
b Have they been working here very long?
No, they have not (haven't) been working here very long.
c Has Alan been climbing mountains since 2000?
No, Alan has not (hasn't) been climbing mountains since 2000.
d Has Jim been taking photos all afternoon?
No, Jim has not (hasn't) been taking photos all afternoon.
e Has Sue been playing the guitar for two years?
No, Sue has not (hasn't) been playing the guitar for two years.
f Has Colin been playing football since breakfast?
No, Colin has not (hasn't) been playing football since breakfast.

2
b The sun has been shining since early morning.
c We have been lying in the garden for three hours.
d Freddy has been learning irregular verbs for ten minutes.
e It has been raining for four days now. What a holiday!
f Alison and Jack have been playing tennis for two hours.
g George has been downloading files from the Internet since 5 o'clock.
h Mrs Pryce has been trying to phone her friend in the USA for 30 minutes, but she can't get through.

Will- und *Going to*-Futur

Will-Futur

In bejahten Aussagen bilden wir das *will*-Futur mit *will* + Infinitiv des Vollverbs. Es hat für alle Personen die gleiche Form.

Um die Verneinung zu bilden, setzen wir *not* unmittelbar nach *will*.
Beachte: Die Kurzform von *will not* ist *won't*.
In future a good education ***will become*** *even more important.*
In Zukunft wird eine gute Schulausbildung noch wichtiger werden.

I expect our team ***will win.***
Ich erwarte, dass unsere Mannschaft gewinnen wird.

Mary thinks it ***will snow*** *tomorrow.*
Mary meint, dass es morgen schneien wird.

Ben hopes Dad ***will not/won't be*** *angry with him.*
Ben hofft, dass Dad nicht böse auf ihn sein wird.

It's raining. ***Will*** *you* ***lend*** *me an umbrella, please?*
Es regnet. Werden Sie mir bitte einen Schirm ausleihen?

Gebrauch

Das *will*-Futur benutzen wir für zukünftige Situationen/Ereignisse, die höchstwahrscheinlich eintreten werden, Erwartungen, Voraussagen und Hoffnungen, spontane Entscheidungen.

Daher kommt das *will*-Futur mit den folgenden einleitenden Verben besonders häufig vor:
believe (glauben)
expect (erwarten)
hope (hoffen)
suppose (vermuten)
think (denken)

Going to-Futur

In bejahten Aussagen bilden wir das *going to*-Futur mit *am/is/are* + *going to* + Infinitiv des Vollverbs.
Beachte: *Going to* und der Infinitiv des Vollverbs bleiben bei allen Personen unverändert.

Um die Verneinung zu bilden, setzen wir *not* unmittelbar nach *am/is/are*.

Um Fragen zu bilden, tauschen wir *am/is/are* und das Subjekt aus.
Kate ***is going to buy*** *a new guitar.*
Kate hat vor, eine neue Gitarre zu kaufen.

Helen and Robin ***are going to marry.***
Helen und Robin planen zu heiraten.

*Look at the sky. It'****s going to rain.***
Schau dir den Himmel an! Es wird bald regnen.

*I'****m not going to lend*** *Tom my CDs.*
Ich werde Tom meine CDs nicht ausleihen.

Are you going to invite Tom *to your party?*
Wirst du Tom zu deiner Party einladen?

Gebrauch

Wir benutzen das *going to*-Futur für zukünftige Pläne und Absichten. Wenn wir etwas vorhaben oder etwas beabsichtigen, dann benutzen wir im Englischen das *going to*-Futur.

Wir benutzen das *going to*-Futur auch für Situationen und Ereignisse, die bald eintreten werden. Dies ist besonders der Fall, wenn im Moment des Sprechens bereits eindeutige Anzeichen gegeben sind.

Überprüfe hier, ob das Wissen sitzt

1 Schreibe auf, was sich die Personen für das Wochenende vorgenommen haben.

a Tom ______________________ his bike. (clean)

b Ann and Robert ______________________ to the cinema. (go)

c Ron ______________________ football. (play)

d The Simons ______________________ the Parkers. (visit)

2 Setze die angegebenen Verben ein. Benutze dabei nur das *will-future,* und zwar in der Langform.

a I will see (see) you later, Amy.

b Take a coat. It ______________________ (be cold) today.

c Don't worry, I ______________________ (help) you.

d The teachers ______________________ (be) at the form party.

e Kirsty ______________________ (not come) to school without her uniform again. If she does, she ______________________ (get) into trouble.

f We must go now or we ______________________ (miss) the train.

3 Übersetze. Verwende dabei das *will-future.*

a Ich werde nicht vergessen, dich morgen anzurufen.

____

b Das Fußballspiel wird nicht stattfinden.

____

c Ich hoffe, die Preise werden nicht steigen *(rise).*

____

4 Benutze das *will*- bzw. das *going to-future,* um die Sätze mit den angegebenen Verben zu vervollständigen.

a What will happen (happen) if Tom is late again?

b Bob is going to have (have) a party on his birthday.

c Kirsty ____________ (be) 14 tomorrow.

d I ____________ (not buy) Adam any more sweets.

I ____________ (give) him apples.

e Adam ____________ (get) toothache from all those sweets.

f Spooky ____________ (not bark) if you take him out.

g Tweets has no water and no food. Be careful, or she

____________ (be) ill.

h Mr Carter ____________ (give) us a test on Friday.

1 a Tom is going to clean his bike.
b Ann and Robert are going to go to the cinema.
c Ron is going to play football.
d The Simons are going to visit the Parkers.

2 b Take a coat. It will be cold today.
c Don't worry, I will help you.
d The teachers will be at the form party.
e Kirsty will not come to school without her uniform again. If she does, she will get into trouble.
f We must go now or we will miss the train.

3 a I will not (won't) forget to call you tomorrow.
b The football match will not (won't) take place.
c I hope the prices will not (won't) rise.

4 c Kirsty will be 14 tomorrow.
d I am not going to buy Adam any more sweets. I am going to give him apples.
e Adam will get toothache from all those sweets.
f Spooky will not bark if you take him out.
g Tweets has no water and no food. Be careful, or she will be ill.
h Mr Carter is going to give us a test on Friday.

Die Zeitenfolge in *if*-Sätzen

Ein *if*-Satz hat zwei Teile, den *if*-Teil und den Hauptteil.
Es gibt drei Arten von *if*-Sätzen, in denen jeweils andere Zeitformen verwendet werden müssen. Hier werden zwei Arten behandelt:

Typ	*if*-Teil	Hauptteil
1	*simple present*	*will-future*
2	*simple past*	*would + infinitive* (Grundform)

Es spielt keine Rolle, in welche Reihenfolge du die beiden Teile eines *if*-Satzes stellst. Wenn der *if*-Teil an erster Stelle steht, dann trennen wir die beiden Teile mit einem Komma.
If you ***read*** *'Winnetou', you* ***will find out*** *a lot about Indians.*
Wenn du „Winnetou" liest, erfährst du viel über Indianer.

I ***would*** *tell you if I* ***knew*** *the answer.*
Ich würde es dir sagen, wenn ich die Antwort wüsste.

Im *if*-Teil des Satzes steht – je nach Einschätzung des Sprechers – eine erfüllbare oder eine wahrscheinlich nicht erfüllbare Bedingung, im Hauptteil die Folge dieser Bedingung.
Die hier behandelten zwei Arten von *if*-Sätzen werden wie folgt gebraucht:

	if-Teil	Hauptteil	Zeitraum
erfüllbar	*present*	*will ('ll)* + Grundform	Zukunft
unwahrscheinlich	*simple past*	*would ('d)* + Grundform	Zukunft/ Gegenwart

*If Pat is at the party, I'****ll (will)*** *ask her to dance with me.*
Wenn Pat auf der Party ist, bitte ich sie, mit mir zu tanzen.

*We'****d (would) buy*** *a house if we* ***had*** *enough money.*
Wir würden ein Haus kaufen, wenn wir genug Geld hätten.

Überprüfe hier, ob das Wissen sitzt

Vervollständige die *if*-Sätze.

Typ 1

a If the weather _is_ good, we _will go camping_ at the weekend. (be/go camping)

b If I ______________________ a holiday job,
I ______________________ some money. (get/earn)

c The American Indian said, "We ______________________ nothing to eat if you ______________________ all the buffaloes." (have/kill)

Typ 2

d If the taxi-driver ______________________ faster, we ______________________ at the station on time. (drive/arrive)

e A lot of pupils ______________________ better at school if they ______________________ to the teacher. (do/listen)

f If we all ______________________ to understand each other, we ______________________ together peacefully. (try/live)

b If I get a holiday job, I will earn some money.
c The American Indian said, „We will have nothing to eat if you kill all the buffaloes."
d If the taxi-driver drove faster, we would arrive at the station on time.
e A lot of pupils would do better at school if they listened to the teacher.
f If we all tried to understand each other, we would live together peacefully.

46

Past perfect

Form

Wir bilden das *past perfect* mit *had* + Partizip Perfekt (3. Form).
Das *past perfect* ist bei allen Personen gleich.
Bei regelmäßigen Verben endet das Partizip Perfekt (3. Form) immer auf *-ed*. Bei unregelmäßigen Verben hat das Partizip Perfekt eine besondere Form, die du dir einfach merken musst.

Wir bilden die Verneinung durch das Einfügen von *not/n't* unmittelbar nach *had*.

Um Fragen zu bilden, tauschen wir had und das Subjekt einfach aus.
When we arrived, the film ***had*** *already* ***started.***
Als wir ankamen, hatte der Film schon begonnen.

The train ***had gone*** *when I reached the station.*
Der Zug war schon weg, als ich den Bahnhof erreichte.

Jane ***had not/hadn't finished*** *when I saw her.*
Jane war noch nicht fertig, als ich sie sah.

Had *the lesson* ***started*** *when you arrived?*
Hatte die Stunde schon angefangen, als du ankamst?

Gebrauch

Im Englischen wie im Deutschen verwenden wir das *past perfect,* um zu verdeutlichen, dass eine vergangene Handlung bereits abgeschlossen war, als eine andere Handlung anfing.

Zum Vergleich:
When Kim got home, her mother ***went*** *to work.*
Als Kim nach Hause kam, ging ihre Mutter zur Arbeit.

When Kim got home, her mother ***had gone*** *to work.*
Als Kim nach Hause kam, war ihre Mutter bereits zur Arbeit gegangen.

Überprüfe hier, ob das Wissen sitzt

Setze das *simple past* oder das *past perfect* in die Sätze ein. Benutze das *past perfect* mit den unterstrichenen Verben.

a Can you tell us whether the fight ____________ (begin) when you ____________ (arrive), or whether it ____________ (already + start) when you ____________ (get) there.

b Unfortunately, the man ____________ (already + die) by the time the ambulance ____________ (reach) the hospital.

c By the time we ____________ (find) our seats, the concert ____________ (begin).

d After I ____________ (read) that Sara Connors ________ (be) in the film, I ____________ (decide) to go and see it.

e When Mum ____________ (ring) the school this morning, the teacher that she ____________ (want) to speak to ____________ (go) home.

f Before we ____________ (take) Ben to the theatre, he ____________ (never/see) a live performance before.

g I ____________ (just/change) into some clean jeans when the dog ____________ (jump up) and ____________ (make) them dirty.

a began – arrived – had already started – got
b had already died – reached
c found – had begun
d had read – was – decided
e rang – wanted – had gone
f took – had never seen
g had just changed – jumped up – made

47

Das Passiv

This car ***is made*** *in China.*
Dieses Auto wird in China hergestellt.

Cars ***were invented*** *many years ago.*
Autos wurden vor vielen Jahren erfunden.

The puppies ***have not been sold*** *yet.*
Die Welpen sind noch nicht verkauft worden.

Was *this house* ***built*** *by your parents?*
Wurde dieses Haus von deinen Eltern gebaut?

■ Form

In den Sätzen oben sind *is made, were invented, have not been sold* usw. Formen des Passivs.

Wir bilden die Passivzeit mit einer Form von *be* und dem Partizip Perfekt (3. Form).
Hier ist eine Übersicht der gängigsten Zeiten:

Zeit	Form von *be*	Partizip Perfekt
simple present	*am/is/are*	*made*
present progressive	*am/is/are being*	*made*
simple past	*was/were*	*shown*
past progressive	*was/were being*	*shown*
present perfect	*have/has been*	*taught*
past perfect	*had been*	*taught*
will-Futur	*will be*	*played*
going to-Futur	*am/is/are going to be*	*played*

Wir bilden die Verneinung durch das Einfügen von *not/n't* genau wie bei dem Verb *be*.

Um Fragen zu bilden, tauschen wir die Form von *be* und das Subjekt einfach aus.

Gebrauch

Ist der Verursacher einer Handlung unbekannt oder zweitrangig, verwenden wir das Passiv. Die Tat – also nicht der Verursacher – steht im Vordergrund.

Beachte: Wir benutzen das Passiv im Englischen viel häufiger als im Deutschen. Oft verwenden wir im Deutschen das Aktiv mit „man", wenn wir im Englischen das Passiv gebrauchen:

Goulash ***is*** often ***eaten*** with rice.
Oft isst man Gulasch mit Reis.

Überprüfe hier, ob das Wissen sitzt

1 Vervollständige den folgenden Bericht, indem du *is/are* + Partizip Perfekt (3. Form) einsetzt.

Do you know how a hit record *is made* (make)? Well, first the song ____________ (write) and a good group ____________ (found). Sometimes the singers ____________ (know), but quite often they ____________ (not know). Then the song ____________ (sing) without the band. Only the words ____________ (record). If the group isn't very good, the tape ____________ (improve) by studio technicians. Later a professional band ____________ (ask) to fill in the music. The music ____________ (sometimes/play) by very good musicians from symphony orchestras. Then all the radio stations ____________ (give) a copy of the new record. They ____________ (often/pay) a lot of money to play it. If the record is a success, it ____________ (sell) in all the record shops.

2 Setze die angegebenen Verben ein. Verwende dabei die Passivformen des *simple past*.

Yesterday there was nearly a tragedy in Duke Street. Five-year old Mandy Copper *was hit* (hit) by a car and ____________ (throw) into the path of a bus coming in the other direction. Luckily, nothing happened to Mandy. She was small enough to go between the wheels of the bus. The car driver did not stop, but the car ____________ ____________ (soon/find) by the police. It ____________ ____________ (hid) in a garage in Rose Lane.

The owner of the car ____________________ (take) to the police station, but he ____________________ (allow) to go home again. Someone had stolen his car early yesterday morning. Mandy ____________________ (drive) to hospital in a police car. Doctors said last night that she was "as well as ____________________ (can expect)". They added, however, that she ____________________ (not injure seriously).

1 Do you know how a hit record is made? Well, first the song is written and a good group is found. Sometimes the singers are known, but quite often they are not known. Then the song is sung without the band. Only the words are recorded. If the group isn't very good, the tape is improved by studio technicians. Later a professional band is asked to fill in the music. The music is sometimes played by very good musicians from symphony orchestras. Then all the radio stations are given a copy of the new record. They are often paid a lot of money to play it. If the record is a success, it is sold in all the record shops.

2 Five-year old Mandy Copper (was hit) by a car and was thrown into the path of a bus coming in the other direction. (...) The car driver did not stop, but the car was soon found by the police. It was hidden in a garage in Rose Lane.
The owner of the car was taken to the police station, but he was allowed to go home again. Someone had stolen his car early yesterday morning. Mandy was driven to hospital in a police car. Doctors said last night that she was "as well as could be expected". They added, however, that she was not seriously injured.

Der *by-agent*

Möchten wir den Verursacher einer Handlung in einem Passivsatz doch erwähnen, verwenden wir einen *by-agent*.

Der *by-agent* ist meist eine namentlich erwähnte Person bzw. Gruppe oder nennt die sachliche Ursache eines Ereignisses.
Beachte: Der *agent* wird immer mit *by* eingeleitet.
The Harry Potter books were written ***by J. K. Rowling.***
Die Harry-Potter-Bücher wurden von J. K. Rowling geschrieben.

The first car was made ***by Carl Benz.***
Das erste Auto wurde von Carl Benz hergestellt.

The crash was caused ***by a bird.***
Der Absturz wurde durch einen Vogel verursacht.

Überprüfe hier, ob das Wissen sitzt

Schreibe die Sätze ins Passiv um. Benutze einen *by-agent* nur, wenn es wirklich notwendig oder von Interesse ist.

a Someone has stolen Ben's bike.

____

b Carl Benz invented the motor car.

____

c Did Columbus or Ericson discover America?

____

d They built this church in 1556.

____

e German scientists made the first rocket.

____

f Has someone taken your coat by mistake?

____

g You can buy stamps at that kiosk.

____

h Somebody left the TV on last night.

____

a Ben's bike has been stolen.
b The motor car was invented by Carl Benz.
c Was America discovered by Columbus or Ericson?
d This church was built in 1556.
e The first rocket was made by German scientists.
f Has your coat been taken by mistake?
g Stamps can be bought at that kiosk.
h The TV was left on last night.

49

Passivsätze mit Modalverben und mit zwei Objekten

Passivsätze mit Modalverben

Mit modalen Hilfsverben werden Passivsätze so gebildet:

Subjekt	Modalverb	*be*	3. Form	andere Teile
The bike	*must*	*be*	*returned*	*by 6.*
Drinks	*can*	*be*	*bought*	*at the kiosk.*
Cars	*should not*	*be*	*parked*	*here.*

Nach dem modalen Hilfsverb folgen der Infinitiv von *be (ohne to!)* und die 3. Form (das Partizip Perfekt) des Vollverbs.

Books ***must be brought back*** *within 14 days.*
Bücher müssen binnen 14 Tagen zurückgebracht werden.

Tickets ***can only be bought*** *from ticket machines.*
Fahrkarten können nur an Fahrkartenautomaten gekauft werden.

Cars ***should not be parked*** *on the pavement.*
Autos sollten nicht auf dem Bürgersteig abgestellt werden.

Can *drinks* ***be taken*** *into the stadium?*
Können Getränke in das Stadion mitgenommen werden?

Passivsätze mit zwei Objekten

Somebody sent ***Kim a nasty letter.***
Jemand schickte Kim einen bösen Brief.

Kim *was sent* ***a nasty letter.***
Kim wurde ein böser Brief geschickt.

Der erste Satz oben ist Aktiv. Das Verb *send* hat jedoch zwei Objekte, nämlich ein direktes Objekt – *a nasty letter (wen/was)* und ein indirektes Objekt – *Kim (wem/was).*

Soll das indirekte Objekt – also der Empfänger – im Vordergrund stehen, dann können wir einen Passivsatz bilden.

Dies erfolgt, indem das indirekte Objekt *(Kim)* zum Subjekt des Passivsatzes wird. Das direkte Objekt *(a nasty letter)* bleibt dabei als einziges Objekt des Passivsatzes erhalten.

Geläufige Verben, die oft zwei Objekte haben, sind:

	Subjekt	Verb	indirektes Objekt	direktes Objekt
ask	*The teacher*	*asked*	*Clare*	*a question.*
	Der Lehrer	stellte	Clare	eine Frage.
give	*Joe*	*gave*	*Clare*	*a kiss.*
	Joe	gab	Clare	einen Kuss.
promise	*Joe's dad*	*promised*	*him*	*a laptop.*
	Joes Papa	versprach	ihm	einen Laptop.
send	*They*	*sent*	*her*	*a present.*
	Sie	schickten	ihr	ein Geschenk.
show	*The teacher*	*showed*	*the class*	*a movie.*
	Der Lehrer	zeigte	der Klasse	einen Film.
tell	*Clare*	*told*	*Kim*	*a joke.*
	Clare	erzählte	Kim	einen Witz.

Überprüfe hier, ob das Wissen sitzt

1 Vervollständige die Sätze mit Passivformen. Benutze immer ein modales Hilfsverb.

You can get advice about car security from the police.

Advice about car security can be got from the police.

a Drivers and passengers must wear seatbelts when the car is moving.

______________________________ when the car ist moving.

b You may not park cars on cycle paths.

______________________________ on cycle paths.

c You must activate some anti-theft systems with a special code.

____

______________________________ with a special code.

d People should not hide expensive cameras under seats.

______________________________ under seats.

e You should never leave car papers in cars or thieves might steal them.

______________________________ in cars or

______________________________.

f You must never lock dogs in cars during hot weather.

____

in cars during hot weather.

g Drivers should never put children's safety seats opposite airbags.

____

______________________________ opposite airbags.

2 Stelle die Sätze ins Aktiv bzw. Passiv wie im Beispiel.

Harry gave Wendy a kiss. Wendy was given a kiss by Harry.

a I was asked the way by a driver.

____

b Carr & Co offered my brother a job.

____

c Julie promised Alan an ice-cream.

____

1 a Seatbelts must be worn when the car is moving.
b Cars may not be parked on cycle paths.
c Some anti-theft systems must be activated with a special code.
d Expensive cameras should not be hidden under seats.
e Car papers should never be left in cars or they might be stolen.
f Dogs must never be locked in cars during hot weather.
g Children's safety seats should never be put opposite airbags.

2 a A driver asked me the way.
b My brother was offered a job by Carr & Co.
c Alan was promised an ice-cream by Julie.

50

Formen des Infinitivs und der Infinitiv nach bestimmten Verben

Mit Ausnahme der modalen Hilfsverben – *can, must, should* usw. – können alle Verben den Infinitiv bilden, entweder mit oder ohne *to.*
Wir benutzen den Infinitiv mit *to* nach vielen Vollverben.
Den Infinitiv ohne *to* verwenden wir nach Modalverben.
Kim ***wants to buy*** *a pullover.*
Kim will einen Pulli kaufen.

We ***must save*** *money.*
Wir müssen Geld sparen.

Wir bilden den Infinitiv Passiv mit *be* + Partizip Perfekt (3. Form). Wir benutzen den Infinitiv Passiv mit *to* und ohne *to* genau wie den Infinitiv Aktiv.
Joe ***wants*** *his bike* ***to be repaired.***
Joe will, dass sein Rad repariert wird.

Joe's bike ***must be repaired.***
Joes Rad muss repariert werden.

■ Der Infinitiv nach bestimmten Verben

Oft verwenden wir ein Verb – z. B. *plan* und *hope* – in Verbindung mit anderen Verben.
Kim and Clare ***plan to go*** *camping.*
Kim und Clare wollen zum Camping fahren.

They ***hope to find*** *a campsite in the mountains.*
Sie hoffen, einen Campingplatz in den Bergen zu finden.

Im Deutschen ist dies problemlos, da wir immer den Infinitiv benutzen. Im Englischen dagegen benötigt eine Gruppe von Verben den Infinitiv mit *to* und eine andere Gruppe das Gerundium.

Verben + Infinitiv mit *to*

Da es keine zuverlässige Regel gibt, musst du die folgende Liste auswendig lernen.

afford	*We can't **afford to go** on holiday.* Wir können es uns nicht leisten, in den Urlaub zu fahren.
choose	*Kim **chose to learn** Spanish.* Kim entschied sich, Spanisch zu lernen.
decide	*Joe **decided to buy** a new laptop.* Joe entschied sich, einen neuen Laptop zu kaufen.
hope	*I **hope to arrive** on time.* Ich hoffe, rechtzeitig anzukommen.
plan	*The Hunts **plan to buy** a holiday home.* Die Hunts planen, eine Ferienwohnung zu kaufen.
promise	*I **promise to be** home by 11.* Ich verspreche, bis 11 Uhr zu Hause zu sein.

Überprüfe hier, ob das Wissen sitzt

1 a Welche Verben können den Infinitiv bilden?

____

____

b Wann benutzen wir den Infinitiv mit *to?*

____

c Wann benutzen wir den Infinitiv ohne *to?*

____

d Wie wird der Infinitiv Passiv gebildet?

____

2 Übersetze die deutschen Sätze.

a Ben beabsichtigt, die Universität zu besuchen.

____

b Tom und Helen hoffen, bald in Urlaub zu fahren.

____

c Ich werde versuchen, dich am Wochenende anzurufen.

____

d Sie versprach, mehr zu arbeiten.

____

e Du musst Geld sparen.

____

f Der Tisch muss repariert werden.

____

3 Benutze die richtige Form des ersten Verbs und den *to*-Infinitiv wie im Beispiel.

I meant to work (mean + work) less last week, but I did more hours.

a We ______________________________

(cannot afford + go) on holiday this year.

b ______________________________

(Julie/choose + leave) school last July?

c Joshua ______________________________

(just decide + get) a holiday job.

d You ______________________________

(mustn't refuse + help) people in trouble.

e I spoke to Jeff and he ______________________________

(promise + be) here on time.

1 a Alle Verben mit Ausnahme der modalen Hilfsverben *can, must, should* usw.
b Nach vielen Vollverben.
c Nach Modalverben.
d Mit *be* und Partizip Perfekt in der 3. Form.

2 a Ben plans to go to university.
b Tom and Helen hope to go on holiday soon.
c I'll try to phone you at the weekend.
d She promised to work more.
e You must save money.
f The table must be repaired.

3 a We cannot afford to go on holiday this year.
b Did Julie choose to leave school last July?
c Joshua has just decided to get a holiday job.
d You mustn't refuse to help people in trouble.
e I spoke to Jeff and he promised to be here on time.

51

Der Infinitiv nach Fragewörtern

Im modernen Englisch verwenden wir den Infinitiv mit *to* nach Fragewörtern, statt einen von einem Fragewort eingeleiteten Nebensatz.
Joe can't decide ***what to do*** *at the weekend.*
Joe kann sich nicht entscheiden, was er am Wochenende tun soll.

Can you tell me ***how to get*** *to the station?*
Können Sie mir sagen, wie ich zum Bahnhof komme?

I have no idea ***where to park*** *in Orlando.*
Ich habe keine Ahnung, wo ich in Orlando parken kann.

Zum Vergleich:

Joe can't decide	*what he should do* Nebensatz mit *what* *what to do* *what* + *to*-Infinitiv	*at the weekend.*
Can you tell me	*how I could get to* Nebensatz mit *how* *how to get to* *how* + *to*-Infinitiv	*the station?*
I have no idea	*where I can park* Nebensatz mit *where* *where to park* *where* + *to*-Infinitiv	*in Orlando.*

Überprüfe hier, ob das Wissen sitzt

Übersetze und wähle die Form mit Fragewort und *to*-Infinitiv.

a Mrs Meyer zeigt uns, wie man mit diesem Programm arbeitet.

____

____

b Er wusste nicht, wann er sie anrufen sollte.

____

____

c Ich weiß nicht, was ich sagen soll.

____

____

d Kannst du mir zeigen, wie ich diese Suppe kochen kann?

____

____

e Wir sagten ihm, welchen Schlüssel er nehmen sollte.

____

____

f Mein Bruder lernt, wie er ein Fahrrad reparieren kann.

____

____

a Mrs Meyer shows us how to work with this programme.
b He didn't know when to phone her.
c I don't know what to say.
d Can you show me how to cook this soup?
e We told him which key to take.
f My brother is learning how to repair a bicycle.

52

Formen des Gerundiums

Im Englischen benötigt eine Gruppe von Verben statt des Infinitivs mit *to* die Form des Gerundiums (*-ing*-Form).

Wir bilden die Aktivform des Gerundiums mit dem Infinitiv des Verbs + *-ing*.
*I like **reading**.*
Ich lese gerne.

*He loves **meeting** new people.*
Er liebt es, neue Leute zu treffen.

Die Passivform des Gerundiums bilden wir mit *being* + Partizip Perfekt (3. Form).
*Nobody enjoys **being searched** by security guards.*
Niemandem gefällt es, von Sicherheitskräften durchsucht zu werden.

WISSEN • WISSEN • WISSEN • WISSEN • WISSEN • WISSEN • WISSEN

Überprüfe hier, ob das Wissen sitzt

Trage die richtige Form des Gerundiums ein.

a We really enjoy ____________ (travel) in the euro zone because we hate ____________ (change) money all the time. We think Britain should consider ____________ (join) the euro zone. I know this will mean ____________ (give up) the pound, but so what?

b In 1973, Britain chose to become part of the EU. Now we should stop ____________ (expect) special treatment. Or do we want to risk ____________ (isolate) ourselves? We really must avoid ____________ (let) that happen.

c My sister intends to study American history, so my dad suggested ____________ (go) to a university in the USA. Anyhow, she has decided to apply to Boston University and now she is enjoying ____________ (plan) her course there next October.

a travelling – changing – joining – giving up
b expecting – isolating – letting
c going – planning

53

Das Gerundium nach bestimmten Verben und nach Präpositionen

Wir verwenden einige Verben in Verbindung mit dem Gerundium.
Have you finished doing your homework?
Bist du mit deinen Hausaufgaben fertig?

The man admits taking the money.
Der Mann gibt zu, dass er das Geld genommen hat.

Da es keine zuverlässige Regel gibt, ist es am besten, diese Liste auswendig zu lernen:

admit	*Do you **admit cheating** in the test?* Gibst du zu, dass du in dem Test gemogelt hast?
avoid	*Dad **avoids doing** overtime.* Dad vermeidet, Überstunden zu machen.
deny	*The man **denies taking** the money.* Der Mann bestreitet, dass er das Geld genommen hat.
enjoy	*Do you **enjoy learning** English?* Gefällt es dir, Englisch zu lernen?
finish	*I **finished doing** my homework at 9.* Ich war um 9 Uhr mit meinen Hausaufgaben fertig.
hate	*Clare **hates flying.*** Clare hasst es zu fliegen.
imagine	***Imagine winning** a million dollars!* Stell dir vor, eine Million Dollar zu gewinnen!
keep	*He **keeps shouting** at other drivers.* Er schreit andere Fahrer dauernd an.
like	*I **like watching** TV.* Ich sehe gerne fern.

love	*She **loves shopping.*** Sie liebt es, einkaufen zu gehen.
mention	*Did I **mention meeting** Ann in town?* Habe ich erwähnt, dass ich Ann in der Stadt traf?
mind	*Do you **mind opening** a window?* Haben Sie etwas dagegen, ein Fenster zu öffnen?
miss	*I **missed seeing** this movie last year.* Ich verpasste es, diesen Film letztes Jahr zu sehen.
practise	*He often **practises playing** basketball.* Er übt oft Basketball spielen.
suggest	*Mum **suggests going** shopping this afternoon.* Mama schlägt vor, dass wir heute Nachmittag einkaufen gehen.

Das Gerundium nach Präpositionen

*Kim bought the computer game **after seeing** an ad.*
Kim kaufte das Computerspiel, nachdem sie eine Anzeige gesehen hatte.

*Joe **didn't succeed in winning** the game.*
Es gelang Joe nicht, das Spiel zu gewinnen.

*Kim's not **interested in getting** a dog.*
Kim hat kein Interesse, einen Hund anzuschaffen.

*We're **looking forward to going** to Vienna.*
Wir freuen uns darauf, nach Wien zu fahren.

Verb + Präposition + Gerundium:	be + Adjektiv + Gerundium:	
insist on think of worry about	be afraid of be bad at be crazy about be famous for	be good at be proud of be tired of

Überprüfe hier, ob das Wissen sitzt

1 Wähle die richtige Form und schreibe den Satz vollständig richtig auf.

a Some pupils hate (to do) homework.

____

b Are you worried about (to lose) the match?

____

c Do you like (to read)?

____

d Tony is crazy about (to cycle).

____

e I don't know who (to ask) about this problem.

____

f Is Mandy good at (to dance)?

____

g The boys promised (to try) harder.

____

h The Garners decided not (to go) away at Christmas.

____

i They are thinking of (to move) to Australia.

____

2 Vervollständige die Sätze mit einer Präposition bzw. einem Partikel aus dem Kasten.

after by for in of of to ~~to~~

a I look forward *to* hearing from you shortly.

b Thank you __________ giving me so much of your time.

c Frank joined our club __________ seeing us play last Saturday.

d Nick doesn't like the idea __________ getting a dog.

e Barbara is interested __________ applying for the job.

f I'm looking forward __________ visiting my uncle.

3 Setze die angegebenen Verben in die richtige Form.

a In this mail, they agree ______________ (pay) the bill at once.

b I wouldn't dream of ______________ (do) such a horrible trick.

c We lost the game in spite of ______________ (be) one goal up for 85 minutes.

d My mother always warns us ______________ (talk) to strangers.

e If I were you, I'd think about ______________ (take) an umbrella.

1 a Some pupils hate doing homework.
b Are you worried about losing the match?
c Do you like reading?
d Tony is crazy about cycling.
e I don't know who to ask about this problem
f Is Mandy good at dancing?
g The boys promised to try harder.
h The Garners decided not to go away at Christmas.
i They are thinking of moving to Australia.

2 b for
c after
d of
e in
f to

3 a In this mail, they agree to pay the bill at once.
b I wouldn't dream of doing such a horrible trick.
c We lost the game in spite of being one goal up for 85 minutes.
d My mother always warns us not to talk to strangers.
e If I were you, I'd think about taking an umbrella.

54

Verb + Infinitiv oder Gerundium je nach Bedeutung

Wir benutzen die folgenden Verben je nach Bedeutung mit einem *to*-Infinitiv oder mit dem Gerundium.

■ ***remember, forget***

Wenn es sich bei *remember* und *forget* um die Gegenwart oder die Zukunft handelt, verwenden wir den *to*-Infinitiv.

Bezieht sich der Satz auf die Vergangenheit, benutzen wir das Gerundium.
Remember to buy *some bread, please.*
Bitte denke daran, Brot zu kaufen.

Please ***don't forget to call*** *your aunt.*
Vergiss bitte nicht, deine Tante anzurufen.

Do you remember seeing *Mel Gibson?*
Erinnerst du dich, wie wir Mel Gibson gesehen haben?

Joe ***has forgotten ever dancing*** *with Mandy.*
Joe hat vergessen, je mit Mandy getanzt zu haben.

■ ***stop***

Bedeutet *stop* „kurz anhalten, um etwas zu erledigen", verwenden wir den *to*-Infinitiv.
Bedeutet *stop* „aufhören, etwas zu tun", dann benutzen wir das Gerundium.
We ***stopped to buy*** *some bread.*
Wir hielten an, um Brot zu kaufen.

You must ***stop eating*** *so many sweets.*
Du musst aufhören, so viele Süßigkeiten zu essen.

Überprüfe hier, ob das Wissen sitzt

Lies zuerst den ganzen Dialog durch. Dann setze die angegebenen Verben in der richtigen Form ein.

Peter is trying ____________________ (think) of a present for his mother's birthday.

He is talking to his older sister Molly. "Do you remember ____________________ (give) her that awful scarf last year?" he asked her.

Molly stopped what she doing ____________________ (think)

"Yes, I'd like ____________________ (find) a better present this year," said Molly. "I couldn't stop ____________________ (think) about her face when she opened the present. I'm glad you reminded me. I nearly forgot ____________________ (start) ____________________ (look). I've got an idea. I'll stop ____________________ (work) early tomorrow and we can meet in town."

"Good idea," said Peter. "And we must remember ____________ (buy) a card as well. Mum will be 40 this year."

Peter is trying to think of a present for his mother's birthday. …
„Do you remember giving her that awful scarf last year?" he asked her.
Molly stopped what she doing to think.
„Yes, I'd like to find a better present this year," said Molly.
„I couldn't stop thinking about her face when she opened the present. …
I nearly forgot to start looking. …
I'll stop working early tomorrow …
„And we must remember to buy a card as well. …"

55

Satzstellung in Aussagen

Bejahte Aussagen

Da es im Englischen – ganz anders als im Deutschen – keine Endungen gibt, ist die Satzstellung streng festgelegt:

Subjekt – Prädikat – andere Satzteile

Kommt ein Objekt im Satz vor, steht es unmittelbar nach dem Prädikat:

Subjekt – Prädikat + Objekt – andere Satzteile

Subjekt	Prädikat	Objekt	andere Satzteile
Ben and Kate King	*live*		*in London.*
The Kings	*have*	*a dog.*	
Ben and Kate	*take*	*Luna*	*for a walk every day.*

Die Satzstellung bleibt im Englischen immer dieselbe, auch wenn andere Satzteile vorangestellt werden:

Ben went to the cinema yesterday.
Ben ging gestern ins Kino.

Yesterday Ben went to the cinema.
Gestern ging Ben ins Kino.

WISSEN • WISSEN • WISSEN • WISSEN • WISSEN • WISSEN • WISSEN

Verneinte Aussagen

Um eine Aussage zu verneinen, stellen wir *not* unmittelbar hinter das Hilfsverb.
Kommt kein Hilfsverb in der Aussage vor, benutzen wir *do not/don't, does not/doesn't* bzw. *did not/didn't* als Ersatzverb.
In der gesprochenen Sprache und in E-Mails usw. hängen wir die Kurzform von *not* – also *n't* – direkt an das Hilfsverb.

Subjekt	Prädikat Hilfsverb + *not/n't*	Vollverb	Objekt	andere Satzteile
Luna	*must not*	*lie*		*on the beds.*
Kate	*hasn't*	*finished*	*her lunch*	*yet.*
I	*don't*	*watch*	*TV*	*during the week.*
Ben	*doesn't*	*help*	*me*	*very often.*
The Kings	*didn't*	*buy*	*a new car*	*last year.*

Aussagen mit zwei Objekten

Einige Verben, wie *buy, give, lend* (ausleihen), *send* und *promise* (versprechen) haben zwei Objekte, nämlich ein indirektes Objekt (wem?) und ein direktes Objekt (wen?/was?).
In Sätzen mit zwei Objekten steht das indirekte Objekt (wem?) unmittelbar vor dem direkten Objekt (wen?/was?)

Subjekt	Prädikat	Objekt (wem?)	(wen?/was?)	andere Satzteile
Kate	*gave*	*Luna*	*a steak*	*for her birthday.*
Mary	*sends*	*Kate*	*an email*	*nearly every day.*
The Kings	*didn't buy*	*Ben*	*a laptop*	*for Christmas.*

Überprüfe hier, ob das Wissen sitzt

1 Bringe die Satzteile in die richtige Reihenfolge, indem du sie durch Ziffern kennzeichnest.

a ☐ baking cakes ☐ is ☐ Mrs Nunn

b ☐ a lot of sweets ☐ eats ☐ Adam

c ☐ is playing ☐ Spooky ☐ with Coco

d ☐ Mr Clarke ☐ his new car ☐ is washing

e ☐ is reading ☐ Miss Jones ☐ a book

f ☐ Mr and Mrs Parker ☐ in the garden ☐ are working

2 Bilde aus den Wörtern sinnvolle Sätze über britische Schulen. Schreibe auf ein extra Blatt.

British schools

a all day – at school – British children – have to stay
b a lot of British schools – a special uniform – have
c and – at 4 pm – at 9 am – ends – starts – the school day
d a 90-minute break – for lunch – in the middle of the day – there is
e clubs – have – on Wednesday afternoons – the children

3 Bringe die Satzelemente in die richtige Reihenfolge und bilde vollständige Sätze. Achte auf die Wortstellung und die Zeitformen!

a teach/English/German pupils/Paul/on Mondays

Does Paul teach German pupils English on Mondays?

b his mother/Joe/promise

____

that he would be careful.

c give/her little cat/Mrs Cary/some fresh fish

____

__________________________________ yesterday.

d a card/send/their friends/the Todds

____

____ last Christmas?

4 Setze die Wörter oder Satzteile in die richtige Reihenfolge. Schreibe auf ein extra Blatt.

a lives – in Bristol – Cathy
b jazz dance – her big hobby – is
c a brother – has – and a cat, Tiger – Cathy
d Tim – Cathy's brother – is called
e with Tiger – is playing – in the garden – Cathy
f Cathy – going – to the movies – likes

1 a Mrs Nunn is baking cakes.
b Adam eats a lot of sweets.
c Spooky is playing with Coco.
d Mr Clarke is washing his new car.
e Miss Jones is reading a book.
f Mr and Mrs Parker are working in the garden.

2 a British children have to stay at school all day.
b a lot of British schools have a special uniform.
c The school day starts at 9 am and ends at 4 pm.
d There is a 90-minute break for lunch in the middle of the day.
e The children have clubs on Wednesday afternoons.

3 b Joe promised his mother that he would be careful.
c Mrs Cary gave her little cat some fresh fish yesterday.
d Did the Todds send their friends a card last Christmas?

4 a Cathy lives in Bristol.
b Her big hobby is jazz dance.
c Cathy has a brother and a cat, Tiger.
d Cathy's brother is called Tim.
e Cathy is playing with Tiger in the garden.
f Cathy likes going to the movies.

Fragen

Entscheidungsfragen

Hilfsverb	Subjekt	Vollverb	Objekt	andere Satzteile
Is	*this*		*your dog?*	
Have	*you*	*read*	*the notice*	*over there?*
Can	*you*	*put*	*your dog*	*on the lead, please?*
Does	*your dog*	*stay*		*at home alone?*
Did	*you*	*buy*	*dog food*	*yesterday?*

Diese Fragen sind Entscheidungsfragen, die wir mit *Yes* bzw. *No* beantworten können. Anders als im Deutschen können wir Entscheidungsfragen nur mit einem Hilfsverb bilden.

Ist kein Hilfsverb im Satz vorhanden, dann müssen wir *do/does/did* als Ersatzverb benutzen. Im Englischen gilt *be* immer als Hilfsverb, sogar dann, wenn kein anderes Verb im Satz steht.

Fragen mit Fragewörtern

Bei Fragen, die mit Fragewörtern *(how, what* usw.*)* gebildet sind, steht dieses am Anfang des Fragesatzes.
Frage ohne Fragewort: *Can Bob come round today?*
Frage mit Fragewort: *When can Bob come round today?*

Fragen mit Fragewörtern werden mit einer Form von *to be* oder mit einem Hilfsverb gebildet. Wenn keine Form von *to be* und kein anderes Hilfsverb da sind, steht *do/does* nach dem Fragewort.
Die Satzstellung ist die gleiche wie bei Fragen ohne ein Fragewort.
How do you send *an email?*
Wie schickt man eine E-Mail?

When do we have *English today?*
Wann haben wir heute Englisch?

Where can I get *some stamps?*
Wo kann ich Briefmarken bekommen?

Why are you *late?*
Warum hast du dich verspätet?

How many *DVDs* ***do you have?***
Wie viele DVDs hast du?

How much does *this book* ***cost?***
Wie viel kostet dieses Buch?

Man verwendet *what* meistens, wenn man aus einer unbegrenzten Anzahl von Dingen wählen kann.
Which verwendet man meistens, wenn man die Wahl zwischen einer begrenzten Anzahl von Dingen hat.

	Fragewort	Hilfsverb	Subjekt	Vollverb	andere Satzteile
1	*What*	*are*	*you*	*doing*	*in the garden, Adam?*
2	*Who*	*do*	*you*	*play*	*cards with, Tom?*
3			*What*	*happens*	*at the end of the book?*
4			*Who*	*is coming*	*to your party, Kirsty?*

In den Sätzen 1 und 2 sind *what* und *who* Objekte des Satzes. Wir brauchen immer ein Hilfsverb, also *do, are* usw., um eine Frage zu bilden.
In den Sätzen 3 und 4 sind *what* und *who* Subjekt des Satzes. In diesem Fall brauchen wir kein Hilfsverb, um eine Frage zu bilden.
Wir benutzen *whose?*, um zu fragen, wem etwas gehört.
Whose *book is this? – (It's) Kirsty's.*
Wessen Buch ist dies? – Es ist Kirstys.

Whose *CDs are these? – (They're) Amy's.*
Wem gehören diese CDs? – Sie gehören Amy.

Überprüfe hier, ob das Wissen sitzt

1 Forme die Aussagesätze in Fragen um.

a Spooky likes cats.

Does Spooky like cats? ______

b Mr Carter comes from Liverpool.

______ *from Liverpool?*

c We live in a big house.

______ *you* ______ in a big house?

d The boys always run across the road.

______ across the road?

e Bob can send e-mails to people all over the world.

______ e-mails to people all over the world?

2 Bilde Fragen mit *how, what, when, where, which, who, whose, why.*
In den unterstrichenen Satzteilen steht, wonach du fragen sollst.
Bei den Sätzen mit *who* oder *what* achte besonders darauf, ob es sich dabei um das Subjekt oder das Objekt des Satzes handelt.

a We are having fish and chips for tea today.

What are we having for tea today? ______

b Bob is happy because he has a new football.

______?

c Accidents happen every day.

______?

d I'm reading a book.

______ *you* ______?

e Amy is going out with Kirsty today.

____?

f Kirsty likes the red but not the green blouse.

____?

g Kirsty Nunn lives in Apple Road.

____?

3 Übersetze die unterstrichenen Teile der folgenden Sätze ins Englische.

a Wohnt Kirsty auch in Oak Lane?

____

b Magst du Computerspiele?

____

c Spielen Tom und Bob Fußball oder Handball?

____

d Isst Adam Obst oder Süßigkeiten?

____

1 b Does Mr Carter come from Liverpool?
c Do you live in a big house?
d Do the boys always run across the road?
e Can Bob send e-mails to people all over the world?
2 b Why is Bob happy?
c What happens every day?
d What are you doing?
e Who is going out with Kirsty today?
f Which blouse does Kirsty like?
g Where does Kirsty Nunn live?
3 a Does Kirsty live
b Do you like
c Do Tom and Bob play
d Does Adam eat

57

Aufforderungen

Bejahte Aufforderungen haben dieselbe Form wie der Infinitiv ohne *to.*

Bei verneinten Aufforderungen stellen wir *do not/don't* unmittelbar vor den Infinitiv ohne *to.* Da verneinte Aufforderungen mit *do not* sehr streng wirken, benutzen wir normalerweise die Kurzform *don't,* die freundlicher klingt.

Möchten wir einen Vorschlag in Form einer Aufforderung machen, benutzen wir *let's* + Infinitiv ohne *to* bzw. *let's not* + Infinitiv ohne *to.*
Keep quiet. *I'm on the phone.*
Sei ruhig! Ich telefoniere gerade.

Wait *in the waiting room, please.*
Warten Sie bitte im Wartezimmer!

Do not forget *to buy some bread.*
Vergiss nicht, Brot zu kaufen!

Don't be *so silly, Ben.*
Sei nicht so albern, Ben!

Let's go *swimming this afternoon.*
Lass uns heute Nachmittag schwimmen gehen!

Let's not watch *TV tonight.*
Lass uns heute Abend nicht fernsehen!

Tipp: Im modernen Englisch machen wir Vorschläge oft auch mit *How/ What about* + *-ing*-Form des Vollverbs:
How about going swimming this afternoon?
Wie wäre es, wenn wir heute Nachmittag schwimmen gehen?

What about not watching TV tonight?
Wie wäre es, wenn wir heute Abend nicht fernsehen?

Überprüfe hier, ob das Wissen sitzt

Bilde Sätze mit der Befehlsform. Einige Wörter müssen hinzugefügt werden. Achte auf Pluralformen.

a Doctor: put out/your/tongue

Put out your tongue, please.

b Teacher: not forget/bring/workbook/next lesson

____

______________________________, please.

c Police officer: get out/your car/and/show/car papers

____

______________________________, please.

d Referee *(hier: Schiedsrichter):* not shout/me/like that

______________________________, please.

b Don't forget to bring your workbooks to the next lesson, please.
c Get out of your car and show me your car papers, please.
d Don't shout at me like that, please.

58

Kurzantworten und Frageanhängsel

■ Kurzantworten

Um die Antwort auf eine Entscheidungsfrage *(yes/no-question)* freundlicher klingen zu lassen, benutzen wir im Englischen Kurzantworten.

Um eine Kurzantwort zu bilden, benutzen wir das Subjekt und die Form des Hilfsverbs, die in dem Fragesatz vorkommen, mit *Yes, ...* bzw. *No, ...*

Das Subjekt einer Kurzantwort ist immer ein Subjektpronomen *(I, you, he, ...)*.

***Are you** in the football team, Ben?* – *Yes, I am.* – *No, I'm not.*
Bist du in der Fußballmannschaft, Ben?

***Does** Kate **do** the shopping on Saturdays?* – *Yes, she does.* – *No, she doesn't.*
Erledigt Kate die Einkäufe samstags?

***Have** you **got** a dog, Mary?* – *Yes, I have.* – *No, I haven't.*
Hast du einen Hund, Mary?

***Does** Mary **have** a sister?* – *Yes, she does.* – *No, she doesn't.*
Hat Mary eine Schwester?

***Can** Tom **speak** German?* – *Yes, he can.* – *No, he can't.*
Kann Tom Deutsch sprechen?

Frageanhängsel

Englische *question tags* wie *isn't it?*, *can't she?* und *was he?* entsprechen den deutschen Frageanhängseln nicht?/nicht wahr?/oder?/oder nicht?

Gibt es ein Hilfsverb im Satz, verwenden wir dieses, um das *question tag* zu bilden.

Ist kein Hilfsverb im Satz vorhanden, benutzen wir *do/does/did* als Ersatz, genau wie bei der Fragebildung.
Linz is in Austria, ***isn't it?***
Linz liegt in Österreich, nicht wahr?

Kate can speak German, ***can't she?***
Kate spricht Deutsch, oder?

Ben wasn't ill, ***was he?***
Ben war nicht krank, gell?

Mary hasn't been shopping yet, ***has she?***
Mary ist noch nicht einkaufen gegangen, oder?

You don't like curry, ***do you?***
Du magst Curry nicht, oder?

They didn't see you, ***did they?***
Sie haben dich nicht gesehen, oder?

The Australians drive on the left, ***don't they?***
Die Australier fahren links, nicht wahr?

Kate went to London yesterday, ***didn't she?***
Gestern ist Kate nach London gefahren, nicht?

Ist das Verb im Hauptsatz bejaht, dann ist das *question tag* verneint und umgekehrt:
Linz is in Austria, ***isn't it?***
Ben wasn't ill, ***was he?***

Überprüfe hier, ob das Wissen sitzt

1 Füge Kurzantworten hinzu. Achte auf Pronomen.

a Do you live in Germany?

Yes, I do. No, I don't

b Have you ever been to the USA?

____

c Is your name Julia Harris?

____

d Did Ben have a holiday last year?

____

e Are Ben and Anna married?

____

f Can Julia speak French?

____

g Did the boys have to go to hospital?

____

h Has the boss gone home yet?

____

2 Bilde die fehlenden Frageanhängseln.

a The Greens haven't got any children, ____________________

b There are 32 pupils in your class, ____________________

c You met those people on holiday, ____________________

d That girl over there is your sister, ____________________

e Chris will be at the meeting on Friday, ____________________ f Don't complain to me. I can't do anything about it, ______________

g You don't know where my keys are, ______________

h Ben doesn't speak German, ______________

3 Übersetze die unterstrichenen Satzteile ins Englische.

a Hyde Park ist in London, <u>nicht wahr</u>?

b Cardiff und Swansea sind die größten Städte in Wales, <u>nicht wahr</u>?

c Claudia kann nicht mit. Sie hat keine Zeit, <u>oder</u>?

d Fast alle Engländer haben ein Auto, <u>nicht wahr</u>?

e Sarah liebt Spaghettieis. – <u>Aber ich nicht</u>.

f Grant wurde nicht in London geboren. – <u>Aber ich</u>.

g Robbie mag keinen Tee mit Milch. – <u>Ich auch nicht</u>.

h Ich war letztes Jahr im Lake District. – <u>Martin aber nicht</u>.

1
b Yes, I have. No, I haven't.
c Yes, it is. No, it isn't.
d Yes, he did. No, he didn't.
e Yes, they are. No, they aren't.
f Yes, she can. No, she can't.
g Yes, they did. No, they didn't.
h Yes, he has. No, he hasn't.

2 Immer mit Komma anhängen:
a have they?
b aren't there?
c didn't you?
d isn't she?
e won't he?
f can I?
g do you?
h does he?

3
a isn't it?
b aren't they?
c has she?
d don't they?
e But I don't.
f But I was.
g Neither do I.
h But Martin wasn't.

Die indirekte Rede: Verschiebung der Zeitformen

Möchten wir jemandem mitteilen, was während eines Gespräches gesagt wurde, benutzen wir die indirekte Rede.
Um zu zeigen, dass wir über etwas berichten, verwenden wir ein einleitendes Verb wie *say, tell, answer, think* usw. Die Anführungszeichen entfallen.
*Kim: "I **bought** a new pullover **yesterday.**"*
Kim: „Ich kaufte gestern einen neuen Pulli."

*Kim **says** (that) she **bought** a new pullover the day before.*
Kim sagt, dass sie am Tag zuvor einen neuen Pulli kaufte.

*Kim **said** (that) she **had bought** a new pullover the day before.*
Kim sagte, dass sie am Tag zuvor einen neuen Pulli gekauft hatte.

Um das Ausgangsgespräch inhaltlich genau wiederzugeben, müssen wir in der indirekten Rede die folgenden Änderungen durchführen:

- Steht das einleitende Verb im Präsens, bleiben die Zeiten des Ausgangsgespräches unverändert.
- Steht das einleitende Verb in der Vergangenheit, verschieben sich die Zeiten.

Übersicht der Zeitverschiebung

direkte Rede	indirekte Rede
Vollverben	
simple present: play, plays *present progressive: am/is/are playing*	*simple past: played* *past progressive: was/were playing*
simple past: played	*past perfect: had played*
present perfect: have/has played	*past perfect: had played*
past perfect: had played	(keine Änderung) *had played*

direkte Rede	indirekte Rede
Hilfsverben	
will-Futur: *will play* *going to*-Futur: *am/is/are going to play*	*would* + Infinitiv: *would play* *was/were going to* + Infinitiv: *was/were going to play*
Modale Hilfsverben	
can: can play *may: may play* *must: must play* *mustn't: mustn't play*	*could: could play* *might: might play* *had to: had to play* *was/were not allowed to: was/were not allowed to play*
should: should play *ought to: ought to play*	*should have* + Partizip Perfekt: *should have played* *ought to have* + Partizip Perfekt: *ought to have played*
could: could play *might: might play*	*could have* + Partizip Perfekt: *could have played* *might have* + Partizip Perfekt: *might have played*

Du kannst dir für die indirekte Rede vier Regeln merken:

1. Alles was *present* ist, wird *past* (bei mehrteiligen Verben das erste Wort):
   is — *was* — *plays* — *played*
   has seen — *had seen* — *is going* — *was going*
2. Alles was *past* ist, geht zeitlich eine Stufe zurück:
   played — *had played* — *was* — *had been*
3. Modalverben gehen zeitlich eine Stufe zurück:
   will — *would* — *can* — *could*
   may — *might* — *must* — *had to*
4. *could, should, ought to, might, would* bleiben unverändert.

Überprüfe hier, ob das Wissen sitzt

Formuliere die direkten Aussagen in die indirekte Rede um. Benutze das angegebene einleitende Verb im *simple past*.

It is September. Peter Hill and Jane Benson are telling their friends about a camping holiday they had in Scotland in August.

a Jane "We drove to Rotterdam and then we took the ferry to Hull in England." (say)

____

____

b Peter "We landed at Hull at 6 in the morning and we left for Scotland immediately." (add)

____

____

c Jane "Peter suggested spending a night in England, but I wanted to get on to Scotland." (tell + us)

____

____

d Jane "Peter finally gave way as long as I did a lot of the driving." (say with a smile)

____

____

e Peter "I found it easy to drive on the left because there was plenty of other traffic." (point out)

____

____

f Peter "Britain is smaller than we thought so we arrived at our camping site near Edinburgh in the afternoon." (tell + Ben)

____

____

g Jane "All the Scots we met were very friendly and they gave us a warm welcome." (mention)

____

____

a Jane said that they had driven to Rotterdam and then they had taken the ferry to Hull in England.

b Peter added that they had landed at 6 in the morning and they had left for Scotland immediately.

c Jane told us that Peter had suggested spending a night in England, but she had wanted to get on to Scotland.

d Jane said with a smile that Peter had finally given way as long as she did a lot of the driving.

e Peter pointed out that he had found it easy to drive on the left because there had been plenty of other traffic.

f Peter told Ben that Britain was smaller than they had thought so they had arrived at their camping site near Edinburgh in the afternoon.

g Jane mentioned that all the Scots they met had been very friendly and they had given them a warm welcome.

60

Die indirekte Rede: Verschiebung der Zeit-, Orts- und Personenangaben

Verschiebung der Zeit- und Ortsangaben

Ähnlich wie im Deutschen ändern sich die Zeitangaben und Ortsangaben nur, wenn sie sich bis zum Zeitpunkt der Wiedergabe (indirekten Rede) auch verändert haben.

Joe: "I want to buy a bike ***today.****"*
Joe said (that) he wanted to buy a bike ***that day.***
Joe sagte, dass er an jenem Tag ein Rad kaufen wollte.

direkte Rede	indirekte Rede
today	*that day*
tomorrow	*the next day*
yesterday	*the day before*
the day after tomorrow	*two days later*
the day before yesterday	*two days before*
last week/month/...	*the week/month/... before*
next week/month/...	*the following week/month/...*
two/... days/weeks/... ago	*two/... days/weeks/... before*
now	*then*
at the moment	*at that moment*
here	*there*
this/these	*that/those*

Verschiebung der Personenangaben

Oft müssen wir Pronomen durch Nomen oder andere Pronomen ersetzen, um für inhaltliche Klarheit zu sorgen.

(Clare) "I will see ***you*** *later, Kim."*
„Ich werde dich später sehen, Kim."

Clare said (that) ***she*** *would see* ***Kim*** *later.*
Clare sagte, dass sie Kim später sehen werde.

Überprüfe hier, ob das Wissen sitzt

1 Ergänze die fehlenden Formulierungen in der Tabelle

	Direkte Rede	Indirekte Rede
	today	*that day*
a		*the next day*
b	*yesterday*	
c	*the day after tomorrow*	
d		*two days before*
e	*last week/month/...*	
f		*the following week/month/...*
g	*two/... days/weeks/... ago*	
h	*now*	
i		*at that moment*
j	*here*	
k		*that/those*

2 Welche Pronomen müssen hier eingesetzt werden?

a Tom: "I am going home now."

Tom said ______________ was going home then.

b Helen: "I have just telephoned ______________."

Helen said ______________ had just telephoned Ben Snow.

c Helen/Tom: "We are playing cards tonight."

Helen and Tom said ______________ were playing cards that night.

d Helen: "I'm doing ______________ now, Tom."

Helen told Tom ______________ was doing the report then.

3 Verwende die indirekte Rede mit den angegebenen einleitenden Verben. Schreibe auf einen Zettel.

Joe: "I saw a cool movie last night." (said)

Joe said (that) he had seen a cool movie the night before.

a	Kim	"We can't come because we are away."	told me
b	Ben	"I'm going to surf the internet."	said
c	Sheila	"I'll never do such a thing again."	promised her parents
d	Clare	"I'm starting to like Joe more and more."	said
e	Joe	"I'm late because the bus didn't come."	told the teacher
f	Julie	"I wish you had told me that before."	said

1 a tomorrow
b the day before
c two days later
d the day before yesterday
e the week/month/... before
f next week/month/...
g two/... days/weeks/... before
h then
i at the moment
j there
k this/these

2 a Tom said he was going home then.
b Helen: "I have just telephoned him."
Helen said she had just telephoned Ben Snow.
c Helen and Tom said they were playing cards that night.
d Helen: "I'm doing it now, Tom."
Helen told Tom she was doing the report then.

3 a Kim told me (that) they couldn't come because they were away.
b Ben said (that) he was going to surf the internet.
c Sheila promised her parents (that) she would never do such a thing again.
d Clare said (that) she was starting to like Joe more and more.
e Joe told the teacher (that) he was late because the bus had not come.
f Julie said (that) she wished I had told her that before.

61

Indirekte Fragen, Aufforderungen und Bitten

Indirekte Fragen

Bei indirekten Fragen unterscheiden wir zwischen Fragen mit Fragewort und Entscheidungsfragen.

Bei Fragen mit Fragewort übernehmen wir das Fragewort, um die indirekte Frage auszudrücken. Das Subjekt steht wie bei Aussagen unmittelbar vor dem Verb und das Fragezeichen entfällt.
Die Tatsache, dass es sich um eine Frage handelt, wird durch das einleitende Verb – meist *asked* – und das Fragewort selbst verdeutlicht.

Bei Entscheidungsfragen benutzen wir *if* bzw. *whether* (ob), um zu zeigen, dass es sich um eine Frage handelt.

Genau wie bei Aussagen müssen wir oft die Zeiten, Zeit-/Ortsangaben und die ursprünglichen Pronomen ändern.
Mit Fragewort:
*Joe: "**Where** is my coat?"*
Joe: „Wo ist mein Mantel?"

*Joe **asked where** his coat was.*
Joe fragte, wo sein Mantel sei.

Entscheidungsfragen:
*Kim: "Joe **have you seen** my coat?"*
Kim: „Joe, hast du meinen Mantel gesehen?"

*Kim **asked** Joe **if/whether he had seen** her coat.*
Kim fragte Joe, ob er ihren Mantel gesehen habe.

Indirekte Aufforderungen, Anweisungen und Bitten

Wir leiten indirekte Aufforderungen mit *asked* bzw. *told* im Sinne von „sagen" ein.
Beachte: Die Verben *ask* und *tell* haben immer ein Objekt. Daher müssen wir die angesprochene Person erwähnen.

Das Verb der direkten Aufforderung erscheint in From des *to*-Infinitivs. Bei der Verneinung setzen wir *not* unmittelbar vor *to*.
Mrs Hunt: "Joe, ***switch off*** *the TV, please."*
Mrs Hunt: „Joe, schalte den Fernseher bitte aus."
Mrs Hunt ***asked Joe to switch*** *off the TV.*
Mrs Hunt bat Joe, den Fernseher auszuschalten.

*Joe: "****Bring back*** *my CDs, please, Grant."*
Joe: „Bringe meine CDs bitte zurück, Grant."
Joe ***asked Grant to bring back*** *his CDs.*
Joe bat Grant, dass er seine CDs zurückbringen soll.

*Coach: "****Don't forget*** *your sport's kit."*
Coach: „Vergesst eure Sportsachen nicht."
The coach ***told the players not to forget*** *their sport kit.*
Der Trainer sagte den Spielern, dass sie ihre Sportsachen nicht vergessen sollen.

Überprüfe hier, ob das Wissen sitzt

1 Schreibe die Fragen in die indirekte Rede um. Verwende dabei *asked* als einleitendes Verb.

a **Mark** "Which team won the match?"

____

b **Ted** "Have you seen my mobile anywhere?"

____

c **Jack** "Did you go to Ann's party last Saturday?"

____

d **Joe** "Are you going to get a holiday job next summer?"

____

e **Julie** "Where do you go to school?"

____

f **Peter** "When does the next train to Atlanta leave?"

____

2 Mr and Mrs Day fahren übers Wochenende weg. Sie sagen Becky und Josh, was sie während ihrer Abwesenheit alles (nicht) machen sollen. Lies die beiden Listen durch und benutze die Buchstaben A bis H, um die direkten Befehle mit den entsprechenden indirekten Befehlen zu verbinden.

1 **Mrs Day** "Don forget to water the plants, Becky."

2 **Mr Day** "Cut the grass, please, Josh."

3 **Mrs Day** "Becky, remember to get some bread."

4 **Mr Day** "Josh, take out the rubbish, won't you?"

5 **Mr Day** "Don't forget to switch off the TV, you two."

6 **Mr Day** "Becky, don't open the door to strangers *(Fremde)*."

7 **Mrs Day** "Josh, help your sister, please."

8 **Mrs Day** "Please don't fight *(streiten)*, children."

A Mrs Day told Josh to help his sister.
B Mr Day told Josh to cut the grass.
C Mrs Day asked them not to quarrel.
D Mrs Day told Becky not to forget to water the plants.
E Mrs Day told Becky to remember to get some bread.
F Mr Day told Becky not to open the door to strangers.
G Mr Day told Josh to take out the rubbish.
H Mr Day asked both not to forget to switch off the TV.

1 a Mark asked which team had won the match.
b Ted asked whether I/you had seen his mobile anywhere.
c Jack asked whether I/you had gone to Ann's party last Saturday.
d Joe asked whether I/you were going to get a holiday job next summer.
e Julie asked where I/you went to school.
f Peter asked when the next train to Atlanta left.

2 1D 5H
2B 6F
3E 7A
4G 8C

Relativsätze

Relativsätze mit *who/that, which/that, whose*

Ein Relativsatz ist ein Nebensatz, der durch ein Relativpronomen eingeleitet wird. Wir verwenden Relativsätze, um den Hauptsatz näher zu bestimmen.

Für Personen benutzen wir *who/that* und für Sachen *which/that*.

Um Besitz anzuzeigen, verwenden wir *whose* für Personen und Sachen unmittelbar vor dem entsprechenden Nomen.
The girl ***who/that won*** *the race is my sister.*
Das Mädchen, das das Rennen gewann, ist meine Schwester.

The car ***which/that caused*** *the accident was a black convertible.*
Das Auto, das den Unfall verursachte, war ein schwarzes Cabriolet.

Mr Gregg ***is the teacher whose*** *car was damaged.*
Herr Gregg ist der Lehrer, dessen Auto beschädigt wurde.

Is this ***the car whose driver*** *caused the accident?*
Ist dies das Auto, dessen Fahrer den Unfall verursachte?

Relativsätze ohne Relativpronomen

Ist das Subjekt des Hauptsatzes und des Relativsatzes dasselbe *(the dog),* dann benötigen wir ein Relativpronomen.

Ist aber das Subjekt des Hauptsatzes *(the bike)* ein anderes als das Subjekt des Relativsatzes *(David),* dann benötigen wir kein Relativpronomen.

Wir nennen Relativsätze ohne ein Relativpronomen *contact clauses,* da der Hauptsatz und der Relativsatz in unmittelbarem Kontakt stehen.
*The dog **which/that bit** the child was white.*
Der Hund, der das Kind biss, war weiß.

*The bike **David bought** is very fast.*
Das Fahrrad, das David kaufte, ist sehr schnell.

Kommt eine Präposition in einem *contact clause* vor, steht sie unmittelbar nach dem Verb:
*The girl I **spoke to** is Ben's sister.*
Das Mädchen, mit dem ich gesprochen habe, ist Bens Schwester.

*The school we **go to** is in Leeds.*
Die Schule, die wir besuchen, ist in Leeds.

*The firm he **works at** is American.*
Die Firma, in der er arbeitet, ist amerikanisch.

Überprüfe hier, ob das Wissen sitzt

1 Opa Peter zeigt seinen Kindern alte Fotos. Er gibt zu jedem Foto eine Erklärung. Verbinde die Sätze mithilfe eines Relativpronomens.

a This is a little town in Cornwall. Its name is Portewe.

This is a little town in Cornwall *whose name is Portewe*.

b This is Uncle Benjamin. His family has lived in Norfolk for over 300 years.

This is Uncle Benjamin ______________________ in Norfolk for over 300 years.

c These are some friends. Their home is in Ulster.

These are some friends ______________________ in Ulster.

d This is a part of Scotland. It has beautiful mountains and lakes.

This is a part of Scotland ______________________ beautiful mountains and lakes.

e This is York. The city gets a lot of visitors every year.

This is York, the city ______________________ a lot of visitors every year.

f This is Gareth Evans. His home is in Wales.

This is Gareth Evans ______________________ in Wales.

g This is my school. Its buildings are very old.

This is my school ______________________ very old.

h And this is my first girlfriend. Her name was Liz.

This is my first girlfriend ______________________ Liz.

2 Wo notwendig, setze ein Relativpronomen ein. Sonst lass die Sätze als *contact clauses* stehen.

a Hollywood is a place _that_ interests many people.

b People __________ live in Hollywood are not all film stars.

c Many films __________ were made here have become big hits.

d A film __________ many people enjoyed was 'Mission Impossible.'

e An actor __________ is now very popular is Tom Cruise.

f Yesterday I saw the actress __________ made this film.

g What is the city __________ the Beatles came from?

h 'Drowned world' is a song __________ Madonna sings.

i A TV series __________ was very popular is 'Friends'.

j The milk __________ I drank was off *(schlecht)*.

k The girl __________ Anna met is Clara.

l Do you know the man __________ says things __________ nobody understands?

1 b This is Uncle Benjamin whose family has lived in Norfolk for over 300 years.
c These are some friends whose home is in Ulster.
d This is a part of Scotland which/that has beautiful mountains and lakes.
e This is York, the city which gets a lot of visitors every year.
f This is Gareth Evans whose home is in Wales.
g This is my school whose buildings are very old.
h This is my first girlfriend whose name was Liz.

2 b who/that c which/that
d — e who/that
f who/that g —
h — i which/that
j — k —
l who/that; —

if-Sätze

Allgemeine Merkmale

Ein *if*-Satz besteht aus zwei Teilen, einem *if*-Teil und einem Hauptteil. Der *if*-Teil drückt eine Bedingung aus, der Hauptteil eine Folge.
Der *if*-Teil kann vor oder nach dem Hauptteil stehen. Steht er aber an erster Stelle, trennen wir ihn von dem Hauptteil durch ein Komma.
Je nach Sinn können wir den *if*-Teil, den Hauptteil oder beide Teile verneinen.

Bei Fragen können wir nur den Hauptteil als Frage bilden. Dann steht der Hauptteil vor dem *if*-Teil an erster Stelle.

Je nach Sinn können wir andere Hilfsverben im Hauptteil verwenden.
If it ***rains,*** *I* ***will stay*** *at home.*
Wenn es regnet, werde ich zu Hause bleiben.

I ***will stay*** *at home if it* ***rains.***
Ich werde zu Hause bleiben, wenn es regnet.

I ***won't stay*** *at home if it* ***doesn't rain.***
Ich werde nicht zu Hause bleiben, wenn es nicht regnet.

Will you ***stay*** *at home if it rains?*
Wirst du zu Hause bleiben, wenn es regnet?

If it's sunny, we ***can go*** *for a walk.*
Wenn es sonnig ist, können wir einen Spaziergang machen.

You ***should call*** *a doctor if you don't feel well.*
Du solltest einen Arzt rufen, wenn du dich schlecht fühlst.

Die Zeitenfolge in *if*-Sätzen

Es gibt drei Typen von *if*-Sätzen mit unterschiedlichen Zeitenfolgen:

	If-Teil	Hauptteil
Typ 1	*if + simple present*	*will*-Futur *can* *may* *should*
Typ 2	*if + simple past*	*would* + Infinitiv *could* *might* *should*
Typ 3	*if + past perfect*	*would have* + Partizip Perfekt *could have* *might have* *should have*

*If you **train** hard, you **will win** the game.*
Wenn du hart trainierst, wirst du das Spiel gewinnen.

*If you **trained** hard, you **would win** the game.*
Wenn du hart trainieren würdest, würdest du das Spiel gewinnen.

*If you **had trained** hard, you **would have won** the game.*
Wenn du hart trainiert hättest, hättest du das Spiel gewonnen.

Überprüfe hier, ob das Wissen sitzt

1 Vervollständige die *if*-Sätze mit dem fehlenden Verb.

a Billy would have won if he __________ (try) harder.

b If Joe worked harder, his teacher __________ (give) him better grades.

c I'd buy a new bike if I __________ (have) enough money.

d If you had got up earlier, you __________ (not miss) your bus.

e If there __________ (be) a cinema in our town, I would go to it.

f If you see Mandy, __________ (you/can tell) her to call me?

g Of course I __________ (help) you if you want.

h We will have a picnic tomorrow if it __________ (not rain).

i __________ (Italy/win) if the referee had not been so unfair?

j Would you visit the USA if you __________ (can)?

2 Verbinde einen Satzteil aus dem Kasten mit einem Satzteil unten, um sinnvolle Sätze zu bilden.

if he sees her	if it snows
if she had asked for it	if we all worked harder
if you had the money	~~I'm sure she'll help you~~
they would have won	we wouldn't have been late
if it had been checked regularly	

a If you ask Helen politely, *I'm sure she'll help you.*

b If the bus had come on time, ______________________________

______________________________.

c Would they pay us more, ______________________________

______________________________?

TESTEN • TESTEN • TESTEN • TESTEN • TESTEN • TESTEN • TESTEN

d Tom will give Anna your message ______________________________

____.

e If they had scored one more goal, ______________________________

____.

f We will go skiing at the weekend ______________________________

____.

g Would you buy a house ______________________________

____?

h The plane wouldn't have crashed ______________________________

____.

i Anna would have got the job ______________________________

____.

1
a ... if he had tried harder.
b ... his teacher would give him better grades.
c ... if I had enough money.
d ... you would not have missed your bus.
e If there were a cinema in our town ...
f ... can you tell her to call me?
g Of course I will help you ...
h ... if it doesn't rain.
i Would Italy have won ...
j ... if you could?

2
b we wouldn't have been late
c if we all worked harder
d if he sees her
e they would have won
f if it snows
g if you had the money
h if it had been checked regularly
i if she had asked for it

64

Der Gebrauch von *if*-Sätzen

Die drei Typen von *if*-Sätzen unterscheiden sich gemäß der Wahrscheinlichkeit der zu erwartenden Folge, und zwar:

Typ 1	Die Folge ist sicher oder mindestens sehr wahrscheinlich.
Typ 2	Die Folge ist möglich, aber eher unwahrscheinlich.
Typ 3	Die Folge ist völlig unmöglich, da wir das Ergebnis schon kennen.

1 *If I **find** a job, I **will/can ... leave** school.*
Wenn ich einen Job finde, werde/kann ... ich die Schule verlassen.

2 *If I **found** a job, I **would/could/... leave** school.*
Wenn ich einen Job fände, würde/könnte/... ich die Schule verlassen.

3 *If I **had found** a job, I **would/could/... have** left school.*
Wenn ich einen Job gefunden hätte, hätte/könnte ich die Schule verlassen/verlassen können/...

Überprüfe hier, ob das Wissen sitzt

Vervollständige diese *if*-Sätze. Lies dir vorher den deutschen Satz gut durch und entscheide, um welchen *if*-Satztyp es sich jeweils handelt.

a If Mr Blake *gives* (give) her a job this summer, Alison *will work* (work) during the holidays.
Alison wird bestimmt arbeiten, falls Mr Blake ihr eine Stelle gibt, also handelt es sich um Typ 1.

b Harry ________________ (have) less serious car accidents if he ________________ (not drive) so fast.
Höchstwahrscheinlich wird Harry trotzdem weiterhin zu schnell fahren, also handelt es sich um Typ ___.

c Pat says she ________________ (go) back to live in Britain if she ________________ (find) a good job there.
Vorausgesetzt, dass sie eine gute Stelle findet, wird Pat mit Sicherheit zurück nach Großbritannien gehen, das ist Typ ___.

d Ms Pratt ________________ (do) interesting History projects with us if we ________________ (behave) better in lessons.
Da die Klasse wahrscheinlich weiterhin den Geschichtsunterricht stören wird, handelt es sich um Typ ___.

e Kelly _______ (buy) that T-shirt if it _______ (be) still there.
Da Kelly das T-Shirt bestimmt kaufen wird, falls es noch da ist, handelt es sich um Typ ___.

b Harry would have … if he didn't drive … (Typ 2)
c Pat says she will go … if she finds … (Typ 1)
d Ms Pratt would do … if we behaved … (Typ 2)
e Kelly will buy … if it is … (Typ 1)

ANHANG

Alphabetische Liste der grammatischen Begriffe

deutscher Begriff	englischer Begriff	Beispiel
abstraktes Nomen	*abstract noun*	*fun, life, technology*
Aktiv	*active*	*Joe's dad **repairs** cars.*
Adjektiv	*adjective*	*Bonzo is a **nice** dog.*
Adverb	*adverb*	*Bonzo runs very **quickly.***
→ Häufigkeitsadverb	*adverb of frequency*	*We **often** watch TV.*
→ Ortsadverb	*adverb of place*	*I live **in York.***
→ Satzadverb	*sentence adverb*	***Of course** I like you.*
→ Zeitadverb	*adverb of time*	*Kim comes home **at 4.30.***
Artikel	*article*	
→ bestimmter Artikel	→ *definite article*	***The** dog is in **the** garden.*
→ unbestimmter Artikel	→ *indefinite article*	***An** apple is **a** kind of fruit.*
Aussage	→ *statement*	
→ bejahte Aussage	→ *affirmative statement*	*Bonzo is the Hunt's dog.*
→ verneinte Aussage	→ *negative statement*	*Ben cannot ski very well.*
Fragewort	*question word*	***Where** is Bonzo?*
Futur	*future*	
→ *going to*-Futur	→ *going to-future*	*We **are going to buy** a house.*
→ will-Futur	→ *will-future*	*I **will see** you later.*

deutscher Begriff	englischer Begriff	Beispiel
Gegenwart → einfache Form der Gegenwart → Verlaufsform der Gegenwart	*present* *simple present* *present progressive*	 *We **go** to school every day.* *Dad **is washing** the car.*
Genitiv → -'s-Genitiv > *of*-Genitiv	*genitive* → *-'s-genitive* - *of-genitive*	 *Kim is **Joe's** sister.* *What's the name **of the town?***
Imperativ (Befehlsform)	*imperative*	***Sit** down and **be** quiet, please.*
Infinitiv	*infinitive*	*We want **to go** home now.*
Konjunktion (Bindewort)	*conjunction*	*We can watch TV **or** play a game.*
konkretes Nomen	*concrete noun*	*car, dog, house, school*
Konsonant	*consonant*	*b, c, d, f, g, h, j, k, l and so on*
Nomen	*noun*	*My **dad** is a **reporter.***
Objekt → direktes Objekt → indirektes Objekt	*object* → *direct object* → *indirect object*	 *Children love **ice-cream.*** *Mum gave **Kim** some ice-cream.*
Partizip Perfekt (3. Form)	*past participle*	***Has** Mum **gone** to work yet?*
Person	*person*	*The first person plural is **we.***

Anhang

deutscher Begriff	englischer Begriff	Beispiel
Personalpronomen → Objektform/-pronomen → Subjektform/-pronomen	*personal pronoun* → *object form* → *subject form*	***We*** *met* ***them*** *in town.* *Ben saw* ***her*** *in town.* ***He*** *plays football.*
Plural	*plural*	*We have two* ***dogs*** *and three* ***mice.***
Possessivbegleiter	*possessive adjective*	*This is* ***my*** *brother, Joe.*
Prädikat	*predicate*	*We* ***are doing*** *our homework.*
Präposition → Präposition des Ortes → Präposition der Zeit	*preposition* → *preposition of place* → *preposition of time*	*The Hunts are* ***in*** *New York.* *We go to school* ***at*** *8.30.*
Pronomen	*pronoun*	***We*** *saw* ***him*** *take* ***it.***
Singular	*singular*	*I ate* ***an apple*** *and* ***a banana.***
Subjekt	*subject*	***My English teacher*** *is quite nice.*
Vergangenheit → einfache Form der Vergangenheit → Verlaufsform der Vergangenheit	*past* *simple past* *past progressive*	*I* ***went*** *to the movies yesterday.* *Kim* ***was cooking*** *the lunch.*
Verneinung	*negative form*	*I* ***don't like*** *fish much.*
Vokal	*vowel*	*a, e, i, o, u*